The Woman of Substance

The Journey to Greatness

BIMPE ISHOLA

The Woman of Substance: The Journey to Greatness
© 2013 by Bimpe Ishola

Published by Eleviv Publishing Group
Houston, TX 77082
www.elevivpublishinggroup.com
1-832-328-7935

ISBN-13:978-0-9886289-7-7
ISBN-10:098862897X

Unless otherwise indicated, Scripture quotations are taken from the NKJV HOLY BIBLE,
"Scripture taken from the New King James Version®. Copyright © 1982 by Thomas Nelson, Inc. Used by permission. All rights reserved."
"Scripture quotations taken from the Amplified® Bible,
Copyright © 1954, 1958, 1962, 1964, 1965, 1987 by The Lockman Foundation Used by permission." (www.Lockman.org)

All the stories in this book are used by permission. To protect the privacy of those who shared their stories with the author, some names and details have been changed.

Cover Design: Tunji Ishola
Printed in the United States of America

Dedicated

To women all over the world
Seeking to use every strand of their God-given potential to
achieve greatness.

And, to my princesses-
Oreoluwa, Odunayo, Boluwatife, and Oluwaseyifunmi -
May you discover and experience the joy, fulfillment, and
dignity of womanhood early.

Table of Contents

Acknowledgements

I love to teach, so I naturally have to read. As I read, I take notes and I keep them. I have notes I have kept for upward of 15 or more years. I never gave writing a book a serious thought until 2009 when a church member asked me when I am going to publish my books! Thereafter, I started attempting to write.

The inspiration for this book was sudden, forceful and clearly divine. I am most grateful to God, my Lord and Savior, and I give Him all the glory for the inspiration, encouragement and all the needed help which He sent my way as I wrote this book. I am greatly indebted to God for my salvation and diverse opportunities which He brought my way to facilitate my growth in Him.

Those 'needed help' include many people who came along with me as I wrote this book. Top on the list is my husband, Pastor Daniel Ishola, and our princesses -Oreoluwa, Odunayo, Boluwatife and Oluwaseyifunmi. For many years you have been my greatest cheerleaders especially in the work of ministry. I am extremely grateful to you for your love, patience and understanding as I juggle many things together sometimes at the expense of your personal comfort.

Next, my appreciation goes to my spiritual parents, Pastor and Pastor (Mrs.) E. A. Adeboye, the General Overseer of The

Redeemed Christian Church of God Worldwide from whom I learned to love and serve God joyfully. I also wish to thank the following people who in various ways have positively influenced my life: my Chairman, Pastor James Fadele and his wife Pastor (Dr.) Manita Fadele, for their on-going support and encouragement, Pastor & Pastor (Mrs.) Bayo Adeyokunnu, Pastor Tola Odutola, Pastor Ghandi Olaoye, Pastor Tosin Macauley, Pastor Tyla Dough, Pastor Caleb Gbenro, Pastors Les & Sheila Bowling, Pastor Niran Fafowora, Pastor & Pastor (Mrs.) Kamal Sanusi, Mrs. O.S Olasehan, and Colonel K. Adesope - you have individually played pivotal roles in my life and ministry and I am very grateful to you.

I'd also like to thank 'Uncle T' and Omolara for their utmost confidence in me which is a solid encouragement. To Barnabas Olaniru who originally gave me the push to write, to Karen Hart, who rekindled the dream late last year by reminding me about the book I was writing, to Quineta and Amina who typed my manuscripts, my friends Bisi Atinmo who edited the book, Moji Oyedele and Tokunbo Oyejola for their prayerful support, Vivian Elebiyo-Okojie who 'did all the work' to the point of publishing the book, my siblings –The Adesokan Clan- and finally my church family members at Ikorodu, Nigeria and here in Columbus, Ohio - most especially all the women that God has used to be a blessing to me as we share and fellowship together, I say 'THANK YOU.'

Commentaries

A Woman of Substance is a woman who is visionary, focused, professional, and deeply spiritual (i.e. connected to God through Christ). She is a woman who is gifted, hardworking, creative and compassionate, she is a person who is strong and yet exudes a heart of care and compassion. She must be sensitive, eager to serve others, respectful of others and mostly her husband (if married). Must be able to run her own home and uphold family values, She is able to hold up under adversity and is an encourager. A Woman of Substance can become whatever her heart sets out to become with God being the central focus of her life!

Pastor Ghandi Olaoye
Senior Pastor RCCG Jesus House, DC.

A woman of Substance lives by excellence. By the way she carries herself; you will find that without any advertisement, her life makes a statement. In her dressing, her manner of speaking, her spiritual life, especially what you perceive of her in public etc. you can tell that you are not dealing with a mere woman so to speak. Continue to grow in your relationship with God. Do not become obnoxious as some women tend to do once they become seemingly powerful. Never lower the honor and esteem you give to your husband. You are a compliment to and not competition for him. You have no point to prove. Also do not neglect your children and their needs just because you are now well known. God will ask of them from you.

Pastor Margaret Oluwatosin Macauley
Regional Coordinator RCCG North Central Africa

Foreword

'*Is this all?*' This was the powerful question that women were asking between 1957 and 1963. Betty Friedan conducted a nationwide research that discovered that this question was uppermost in the hearts of women of that age. Women were questioning the vacuous nature of the role that the society accorded them. Women of that age were experiencing massive identity crisis. There was a stifling construct of the feminine role. This construct created a generation of depressed and desperately unhappy women who became the fodder of the feminist movement and eventually became instrumental in the re-imagining and total alteration of the American family landscape.

It is an extremely unwise person who will question the impact of Betty Friedan. Her book, *The Feminine Mystique* has been described as the 'impetus for the second wave of the feminist movement.' She, along with Pauli Murray, the first black ordained female in the Episcopal Church, went on to start the National Organization for Women. Among many other things, she successfully fought for the extension of the Affirmative Action Bill to Women in 1967 and she was the main force behind the battle that institutionalized abortion in the landmark Roe vs. Wade Supreme Court Judgment of 1973. She was a woman of substance.

We may not agree with Ms. Friedan's conclusion but we cannot question her premises. The Church oftentimes has lagged behind in providing leadership to a society floundering in the midst of confusion, a society asking legitimate questions. This is why this book, *The Woman of Substance: The Journey to Greatness* is a great source of joy. The book addresses the question that was raised by the women of Ms. Friedan's age. The book looks squarely at the face of *'Is this all?'* and answers it with a ringing passionate conviction, *'No, this is not all!'* Rather than give in to the pessimism of feminism, the author of *The Woman of Substance* brings in the ever fresh hope of the gospel of our Lord Jesus Christ.

May I say that historic Christianity has always been a trail blazer in the construct of social justice. The freedom and the value of women was guaranteed by the affirmation and scriptural insistence that *'male and female created he them.'* In this statement at the beginning of the days of man, there was gender differentiation without any unnecessary value demolition. Looking through the scriptures, you see unadulterated commitment to the value of womanhood. Whether one is studying Sarah, whom the angel *personally asked for by name,* or the student is looking at Deborah who led a nation to *a critical victory*; whether you are looking at Mary, the teenager who was greatly honored as the mother of our Lord, God places great value on womanhood. He seeks to convince his world to do the same.

More than any other person, Jesus our Lord validated all the women that came in contact with him. When Jesus said *'virtue has gone out of me'* in Mark 5:30, he was stating that the totality of his nature, the power inherent within him as God, the very nature of the divine, his *dunamis;* has been transmitted from him to a sick woman! What value! What affirmation! What a glorious hope! The essential nature of the Godhead was exchanged on a Judean street between Jesus and a sick woman! If this was so then, how much more so today! The Church of Christ must assist the people of our world to rediscover this value today.

I read through *The Woman of Substance.* I was particularly impressed by the directness and the simple manner with which extremely profound truth was presented. I was impressed by the depth of research (The Ten Cow Woman), the personalized application (Ikorodu Experience), the biblical exegesis and the contribution by matured leaders from various backgrounds.

Let me close by saying that there is a need today for 'Women of Substance' as described by the book. I cannot but reference history again. During the 100 Years of War in Europe, one of the most compelling stories was that of a young peasant girl named Joan of Arc. She got a Divine Vision and mobilized an army to free France from its then invaders. She was captured, tried and burnt at the stake at the age of 19 years; she was absolved of all guilt 25 years later. Nearly 500 years after her death, the Roman Catholic Church canonized her in 1920. One must ask a question: *what kind of life keeps having impact after 500 years?* What kind of impact would we be having many years from now. This is the question that *The Woman of Substance* sets out to answer.

As you read these pages, you will be inspired to be a woman of substance. My prayer is that the passion that guided the writing of this book will serve as a Holy Seed that will keep bearing seed 500 years from now and may your life never remain the same in Jesus name!

Pst. (Dr.) James O. Fadele;
Chairman, The Redeemed Christian Church of God,
North America.

Introduction

This book provides me with an opportunity to testify that God is great, sovereign, undoubtedly loves the unlovable and is a very present help in trouble. In my brief sojourn in life (I turn 52 as I write this book); I have experienced what Apostle Paul described in 2Corinthians 4:8-10.

> *'We are hard-pressed on every side, yet not crushed; we are perplexed, but not in despair; 9 persecuted, but not forsaken; struck down, but not destroyed—10 always carrying about in the body the dying of the Lord Jesus, that the life of Jesus also may be manifested in our body.'*

And, in 2 Corinthians 1:8-11

> *'For we do not want you to be ignorant, brethren, of our trouble which came to us in Asia: that we were burdened beyond measure, above strength,*

> *so that we despaired even of life. 9 Yes, we had the sentence of death in ourselves, that we should not trust in ourselves but in God who raises the dead, 10 who delivered us from so great a death, and does[a] deliver us; in whom we trust that He will still deliver us, 11 you also helping together in prayer for us, that thanks may be given by many persons on our[b] behalf for the gift granted to us through many.'*

I write this book with the assurance that the Father of mercies and God of all comfort will comfort and encourage every woman (and every man) going through any pressure or trouble just as He did for me.

I experienced the height of pressure in the year 2012 to the extent that I plunged into depression; the type psychologists will call clinical depression, but I refused therapy because I knew my God would come through for me. At the height of the pressure, I thought of doing the unthinkable. However, at the end of the long, dark tunnel, light shone. I was lifted, elevated and refreshed! With the benefit of hindsight, clearly the 'pressure' I experienced can be likened to the travail of a woman in labor!

Isaiah 66: 8-9 says:

> *'Who has heard such a thing? Who has seen such things? Shall the earth be made to give birth in*

one day? Or shall a nation be born at once? For as soon as Zion was in labor, She gave birth to her children. 9. Shall I bring to the time of birth, and not cause delivery?' says the Lord. 'Shall I who cause delivery shut up the womb?' says your God.'

At this very moment, I am out of 'labor' and I am bringing forth. Writing this book is one of the 'children' that the travail produced. Glory be to God!

To all my womenfolk or comrades, this book will encourage you to persevere in the midst of trials, tribulations, and sufferings. I remind you of the hymn:

**O my comrades, see the signal, waving in the sky!
Reinforcements now appearing, victory is nigh.**

Refrain:

*'Hold the fort, for I am coming,' Jesus signals still;
Wave the answer back to Heaven, 'By Thy grace we will'*

**2.   See the mighty host advancing, Satan leading on;
Mighty ones around us falling, courage almost gone!**

3. See the glorious banner waving! Hear the trumpet blow!
In our Leader's Name we triumph over every foe.
4. Fierce and long the battle rages, but our help is near;
Onward comes our great Commander, cheer, my comrades, cheer!

This book will equally challenge you to arise in the spirit and discover the hidden substance in you, which is the reason for your existence and the hope for your fulfillment. You will learn practical things you can do on your journey towards greatness. Also, you will have the opportunity to have a glimpse into the minds of a few women who have clearly identified the purpose of their existence and are marching forward, fulfilling it. Young people who are at the verge of making a decision on marriage will find useful hints that will aid their decision.

In *The Woman of Substance – The Journey To Greatness*, you will read not only about the travails of a woman, a child of destiny struggling to discover and come in alignment with her true self in order to fulfill her purpose, you will also read about her victories, joys, challenges, and hopes. I am confident in God that you will be richly blessed as you read on.

Chapter One

My Epitaph: 'A woman who, though started late in life, lived godly and raised many godly women.'

'Though your beginning was small, yet your latter end
would increase abundantly'
Job 8:7 (NKJV)

I cannot remember at what point in my life I got very passionate about issues pertaining to women- their travails, challenges, victories, joys, and empowerment. I remember however, that sometime in November 1998, I stumbled on a copy of Charisma Christian Magazine. The lead story was on Joyce Meyer and it claimed that "America's most popular women minister is teaching thousands how to overcome stress, fear, and discouragement." I read the article and I was astounded as well as challenged. I was astonished by her style of ministry, her forthrightness, her openness, and the enormous impact she was having on people. I was challenged and encouraged by her boldness and influence. As I read her story further, something reared up within me and I made a decision to become a woman of impact in my generation as well.

I began dreaming about ministering to women, even to establish what I named the Dayspring Christian Resource Center sometime in the future. I underlined the statement credited to William Jones (Co-Pastor with Virginia Jones of a non-denominational charismatic church in Haworth, Oklahoma) that Joyce Meyer's teachings on radio (then called "Life In the Word") "makes the bible alive and that we need more women like her; bold speakers who will bring out the truth." There are many other statements which I underlined in the story on Joyce Meyer (I have kept the November 1998 edition of Charisma Christian Magazine till date).

I strongly believe that was the time my very special interest in women affairs was birthed. I have since followed Joyce Meyer's Ministry activities. Joyce Meyer is a very practical, down to earth preacher/teacher of God's word who exemplifies extraordinary simplicity in her teachings. Joyce doesn't mince words or encourage people to feel sorry for themselves; yet her messages are laced with grace. I could relate with some of her experiences.

In 1999, the Lord provided me an opportunity to have direct influence over women when my church asked me to pioneer the establishment of a local parish in Ikorodu town, Nigeria, where I lived. As a female Pastor, my heart was certainly with women and I had lots of opportunities to relate with them, encourage them, chastise them, and befriend them as each occasion dictated.

By divine plan and arrangement, my family and I relocated to the USA in 2003 and our primary assignment was pastoring. As a Pastor's wife, I was directly in charge of the Women Fellowship where I had numerous avenues to support and to positively impact many women. As my interest in women affairs grew, the Lord began to open doors of ministry to me outside of my local assembly at Columbus, OH. I started to receive invitations to minister at women conferences at other churches in USA and Canada!

Sometime in 2005, I penned this statement at the back of my Bible: 'A woman who although started late, lived godly and through God's help, raised many godly women.'

Posterity will affirm this statement. But then, how was *The Woman of Substance – The Journey to Greatness* birthed? This is the focus of the next section of this book.

Birthing: 'A Woman of Substance'

11

'Who has heard such a thing? Who has seen such things? Shall the earth be made to give birth in one day? Or shall a nation be born once? For as soon as Zion was in labor, she gave birth to her children.'

Isaiah 66:8

Birthing *A Woman of Substance* was a long drawn-out process. It all started in 1999 when my church, The Redeemed Christian Church of God, Overcomers Parish Ikorodu, Nigeria, requested me to pioneer the establishment of a local parish named New Wine Parish. It was the third time such a request was being made and I finally consented.

From inception, New Wine Parish was different in concept. The set-up and the unique culture that eventually evolved distinctively set her apart from other parishes.

Soon enough it was time to plan a Women Conference. Ordinarily as the Parish Pastor, my involvement should have been limited to just giving general support to the organizers. However, that was not the case. I was involved at every stage of planning till execution - from deciding the conference theme, who to invite as guest speakers, to the design and printing of flyers. This was my natural constituency and it is something I loved and still love to do. The theme I received for the conference was "A WOMAN OF SUBSTANCE." A senior female pastor in RCCG was invited as the Guest Speaker. Ever since 1999, the theme stuck such that every Women Conference we held in New Wine Parish was themed accordingly.

Taking 'A Woman of Substance' to a Higher Level

'A Woman of Substance' took another dimension in 2003 when the Holy Spirit used it as a platform to address an issue of concern to Pentecostal Christians that lived in Ikorodu, Nigeria. Ikorodu town is notorious for occultic practices, partying and all the vices associated with such. A day is designated to sacrifice to a particular idol called *Eluku*. On such a day, women stay indoors for 24 hours! They are forbidden to step out of their houses. History has it that many years ago, the sacrifice lasted for seven days, but due to civilization, it was reduced to three days and later to one day. Christians living in Ikorodu are usually irritated at such times especially because women could not attend night vigils, if it fell on such a day. It is claimed that some men use such days to perform their adulterous practices.

This particular year the Holy Spirit moved us to stage a spiritual revolt against this evil practice. We organized a march from the city entrance to the city center with the express approval of the king of Ikorodu (Ayangburin of Ikorodu) and prayed over the city, nullifying all demonic activities and establishing the Lordship of Jesus Christ. The queen and her friends were invited to an evangelistic outreach after the march. Held at Ikorodu Town Hall, the outreach took the form of a banquet in order to attract attendance by Ikorodu female indigenes. Giving the meeting a social party outlook, we called for a uniform – white 'iro' and 'buba' with purple headgear! A popular local musician played music which they danced to. However, two powerful testifiers were invited to the event to share their conversion experiences. Also, Pastor (Mrs.) Folu Adeboye, the wife of the General Overseer of The Redeemed Christian Church of God, being the Special Guest Speaker, shared the word of God. Many gave their lives to the Lord at this event and Ikorodu town has never remained the same thereafter! A National Newspaper reported the event, so also a local Christian Magazine called 'Trumpet of Jubilee'. Below is the excerpt from the magazine story.

It was the beginning of a new dawn in Ikorodu on Saturday, 1 February, 2003 at 7:00am when women from various denominations, predominantly RCCG women, gathered and embarked on a spiritual exercise by trekking from the Oba Ayangburen of Ikorodu's palace to Majidun (Ikorodu's gate), stopping at every bus stop to pray, possessing Ikorodu town and its environs for Jesus Christ.

The program, 'Woman of Substance' was initiated by the first female Area Pastor, Pastor (Mrs.) Bimpe Ishola of RCCG, Area 38,

New Wine Parish, Lagos Province 2, with the vision of taking Ikorodu into our hands, starting first with Ikorodu indigenous women and soon all the youth and men joined in as well.

In the plan of God, the time has come for the redemption of homes and family values in Ikorodu, so the program was officially launched on Sunday, 2 February, 2003 at Ikorodu Town Hall. The Holy Spirit really glorified Jesus on that day. Her Royal Highness Olori Muyibat Oyefusi addressed the invitees after which she led a chorus to the glory of God. Also, a Woman of Substance, Sister. Balogun gave a heart touching testimony to the glory of God, affirming the fact that God will surely bring whomsoever he had predestined to be His own to Himself. (Romans 8:29-30).

The Mother of the day, our Mummy G.O. Pastor (Mrs.) Folu Adeboye gave the word of exhortation at the end of which, many people gave their lives to Jesus. Her topic was "A woman of substance demonstrating virtues in her home." The text was taken from Luke 8:1-3.

Substance according to her means something with value, she said after Mary called Magdalene and others were healed of evil spirits and sickness, they were able to serve Jesus (Luke 1:74). The shame of their past was forgotten, all the bad debts were paid and Jesus Christ bought them with a price that no man could afford. He bought them with His blood.

She highlighted some of the virtues that 'you' as a woman of substance must demonstrate in your home. They include:

- *You must have the fear of God and love your neighbor as yourself. Ps. 111:10, Mark 12:31.*
- *You must be a caring mother, and must be able to transfer godliness to your children. Pro. 31:27-29, 2 Tim. 1:5 e.g. Hannah with Samuel who became a great prophet.*
- *You must help your husband to excel. Gen. 2:18.*
- *You must be submissive and be conversant with the word of God. 1 Peter 3:1-6.*
- *You must be longsuffering and be steadfast 1 Cor. 15:58, Gal. 5:22, Ruth long suffered with Naomi and she became the grandmother of Joseph. (Jesus Christ's step-father) if you long-suffer; you will 'long-enjoy.'*
- *You must be hard working, Judges 4:1-10. Deborah was a wife, (possibly a mother), prophetess and a judge who performed legal and military duties in Israel. Her husband Lapidoth was known through her fame. (How about you?).*
- *You must be a giver; remember that God gives seed to the sower. Dorcas was delivered from death because she was a giver and a woman of good reputation. Acts 9:36-42.*

In conclusion, to be a woman of substance is most valuable. You may be an executive, a businesswoman, a prostitute, an addict; Jesus shed His blood and died for all. He is knocking on the door of your heart right now (Rev. 3:20). If you allow the Prince of Peace to come into your life, He will take you from the miry clay to stand you on the solid ground. He will give you beauty for ashes, the oil of joy for mourning, the garment of praise for the spirit of heaviness (Is. 61:3) and instead of your shame, He will give you double honor (Is. 61:7). Praise God. A woman of substance does not want to go to hell. Jesus loves you.

Maranatha! Jesus is Lord.
Bimbo Kelani

That same year (2003), my family relocated to the United States of America. With a growing interest and burden for the woman and doors of opportunities being opened by the Lord to minister to them, *Woman of Substance International* was launched in 2006 as a ministry arm of Glory & Virtue Ministries which was previously inaugurated on August 15, 2005 in Columbus Ohio. The *Woman of Substance International* organizes an annual event where women from all walks of life gather to provide a network of strong support for one another while also receiving individual encouragement as purposes are clarified. At these meetings, women issues are discussed, talents are recognized and applauded while single sisters are mentored on how to prepare for their future homes. The global vision of *Woman of Substance International* is to 'build healthy family relationships through women empowerment.'
The aims and objectives of Woman of Substance International are:

- To bring together in an atmosphere of love and oneness, women of diverse cultures, affinities, and professions for the essence of fellowship.
- To create among women the awareness of the purpose of their creation and the discovery of their personal purposes.
- To synergize, harness and leverage the gifts and talents of the pool of women in fellowship for the benefit of all.
- To promote, build, and restore healthy family relationships.
- To provide spiritual and practical guidance for young adults as they prepare for marriage.
- To work in collaboration with other agencies or ministry groups who share our vision to make our communities safe and strong enough to raise future generations.

Chapter Two

Substance - What is that?

---

*'But we have this treasure in earthen vessels that the
excellence of the power may be of God and not of us,'*

2 Corinthians 4:7 (NKJV)

When I got the idea to write this book, I began to ponder on
some principles especially one about *substance,* and how it
drives our very existence. The English dictionary described
substance as that which is solid and practical in character,
quality, or importance. Without substance, I believe there is
no depth to us as humans. *Substance* is that extra something,
that extra oomph, or "je ne sais quoi" that makes each of us
special. *Substance* makes you stand out; it makes an ordinary
man or woman extraordinary and phenomenal.

Recently, I read an amazing vignette written by an unknown
author of an island in the South Pacific that had a custom
regarding women and marriage. A woman could be
purchased to be a wife with cows. Yes, cows! If the woman

was really beautiful, really attractive and outstanding, she could bring as many as five or six cows. If she was pretty nice, and pleasant looking, she could bring four cows. And if she was average, three cows. There was a man who had two daughters of marriageable age. One was beautiful, and one very plain. He heard of a rich man who was coming to visit because he was interested in one of his daughters. Surely the rich man was interested in the beautiful daughter! And, he further reasoned, the man was rich enough to be at least a "five cow" man, so he thought he would bargain to get as many as five cows for her. The other daughter, the plain daughter, he thought the rich man would not be interested in. She would maybe bring two cows, probably only one and he might have to give her away just to ease his financial burden. However, when the rich man arrived, he showed an interest in the plain daughter. In fact, he wanted to marry her so badly that he paid TEN cows for her! They married, and went on their honeymoon and two years later they came back. How she had changed! Now this woman was well poised, attractive, even beautiful, and quite lovely. It turns out she became a ten-cow woman, because her husband thought he had a ten-cow woman.

The moral of the story is this: The value we place on someone is the value they will probably live up to. The plain looking woman *became* a woman of substance because; high value was placed on her. Not because of her looks or lack of it but because the man that came for her hand in marriage loved her just the way she was. He was willing to offer ten cows to marry her. He placed a high value on the woman she was, and saw much more potential in her than even the woman's father. The man saw *substance*; he saw her essence. That was why she was transformed from plain Jane to beautiful princess. Substance is much more than beauty, it is worth, character, and much more -the life of God inside of us. God Himself talks about beauty being vain but that a woman who loves the Lord shall be praised. The love of God gives substance; it makes your life substantial. Don't get me wrong, looking good is good and women must do their best to take care of themselves. Outward appearance is important, however, it is not nearly as important as the inner man.

Substance refers to the essence, value, worth, quality, physical or material of which a thing consists; the actual matter of a thing as opposed to the appearance or shadow. In seeking a parallel in the Bible for the word *substance*, words like *grace* and *virtue* and *treasure* come to mind.

Grace, aside from being "unmerited favor" of God, also indicates a divine gift or presence that enables a man or woman to do what he or she may not be able to do well outside of "grace". *Grace* refers to all the good gifts we enjoy freely in life. They are so many that perhaps, a summary of them is to affirm that life itself is a gift with all its delights.

Grace also means the secondary gifts we perceive in the skill and intelligence of creatures. It is stated in the gospels that the *boy Jesus grew in grace and favor*, meaning he began to exhibit his unique personality and potential to contribute to his community.

Virtue on the other hand refers to goodness, chastity, good or an admirable quality or propriety. Putting all these together, one may not be far from the truth to state that *a woman of substance demonstrates admirable skill, intelligence and goodness that set her apart from others; she is God's elect lady. A woman of substance is skillful and isn't afraid to use her skills in church and also in the corporate world. She is intelligent and always ready to learn.*

Treasure refers to anything or person greatly valued or highly prized. Men will go to any length to purchase whatever is considered the best. Men have killed, betrayed one another or labored tirelessly in order to acquire wealth or riches. But, there's nothing as valuable as the creation of God! Everything that God created is good and valuable and no one is a better judge of this than God Himself.

'Then God saw everything that He had made, and indeed it was very good.'

Genesis 1:31

What is the worth of a Woman?

In most societies the value placed on women is next to nothing. Some cultures see women as subservient to men and should only be seen, not heard. Turn on your television, watch a movie or even an advertisement, and you will see women both young and old being paraded as sex symbols, or play things. A man wants to sell a car, he hires a lady to dress half naked to appeal to the audience. In Africa, the notion for centuries was that a woman's place was in the kitchen and to make babies.

Growing up with some of these messages makes a lot of women think that their value derives from their looks, their ability to bear children, and such like. Women are certainly more valuable than what the society has tried to define them by. Thankfully, over the last decade there has been a shift in culture; women are not only keeping a home but are making giant strides in predominantly male dominated careers. For instance, the United States recently lifted a ban on women in combat. Unlike decades ago where women were only allowed to working as military nurses, cooks, or in the office, women are now in the war front and could fight just like their male counterparts. Women run multi-billion dollar corporations, are now presidents of countries…etc. We have indeed come a long way.

God has created women for a higher purpose. Our marital status, beauty, and professional career have little to do with our value. A woman of substance must derive her value from what her Maker says about her. God put Adam to sleep rhythmically, and created a woman out of him. Her purpose, worth, and design was determined by God Almighty. He knew all of the intricacies of a woman. We were created as a reflection of God Himself, with all of His abilities, to love, to be creative, and as a strategic partner to our husbands.

The *substance* in a woman is a treasure. Treasures are highly prized and are often hidden or buried deep in the ground. It takes a lot of hard work and effort to dig them out.

'Again, the kingdom of heaven is like treasure hidden in a field, which a man found and hid; and for joy over it he goes and sells all that he has and buys that field. Again, the kingdom of heaven is like a merchant seeking beautiful pearls, who, when he had found one pearl of great price, went and sold all that he had and bought it.'

Mathew 13:44-46

A woman must look deep inside her and go on a journey of self-discovery under the direction of the Holy Spirit in order to know her value and accept her uniqueness. Because it is hidden, and highly prized, this treasure must be located and jealously protected against abuse, misuse, and neglect. The woman must appreciate herself in order for others to accept and appreciate her.

Below are three inspirational write-ups and excerpts that seek to throw light on this crucial issue from different but somehow similar perspectives.

Author Dr. Kristin Beasley, puts it beautifully in an article, 'What is the value that society places on women?

The value of a woman is not based so much on her differing perspectives from that of a man, though they are different. Her value is not rooted in her gender, though her gender is different from man's and should be valued for its femininity and 'femaleness'. Our role, or lack of a role, whether we are married or not, attractive or not, a mother or not, a career woman or not, has little to do with our value. Her value, in my view, is not rooted so much in her role as wife, mother, sister or daughter, though those roles are good and when done well are quite wonderful. But the value of a woman is rooted in the fact that she was made by a God who created her in His image because He loved her, sent His Son to die for her because He loved her, and sealed her, empowered her and gifted her because He thought she was worth it. Her value is most expressed in her identity as a child of God, in her relationship with the Lord of the universe. Woman couldn't be any more valued by God than she already is. She is the crown jewel of His creation! A woman's value, my value (your value) is inestimable, it can't be measured.

And to live up to that is to live life with all the dignity, purpose, and significance granted by God Himself.

Brooke Elise Axtell, an advocate for survivors of sexual and domestic violence and the creator of SHE: Survivor Healing and Empowerment also wrote about the worth of a woman in an article on the internet.

Every-day I am bombarded with conflicting images and media messages that tell me that I am lacking. Relentless consumption framed as self-improvement depends on the lie that we will never be enough. What is lost in the onslaught of ads (and ads posing as television shows) are the authentic desires of women. Diverse women. Women of color. Women who are sexually fluid. Women who know that desire is an unfolding process, a transformative conversation engaging body and soul. When we place the power to define our worth in someone else's hands, we are often told that we only want to be wanted. This artificial script leaves us with an extremely narrow role: to be a pleaser. If we accept society's definition and remain disconnected from our authentic desires, our lives are drained of meaning, emotionally and financially. In this emptied state, we fail to take the initiative to negotiate higher salaries or raise our fees to match our true market value.

We can learn all the techniques available to create mutually beneficial agreements, but cannot even begin a conversation about our value unless we know our worth. As much as we may deny it, our relationship with money mirrors our relationship with ourselves. If we do not build a foundation of self-care, we will never know financial freedom. Do we live beyond our means because we are trying to fill a hunger we cannot name? Do we fail to ask to be well paid because we've never been clear about our own value? What is woman worth? Far more than we've ever imagined.

Yet, another woman has this to say:
The evolution of the woman has been more complex than that of the man. She, more than the man, reflects more clearly the changing values in the society. She, more than the man, is the custodian of the culture. I heard this statement from one of my former bosses, Mr. Ugochukwu Okoroafor: '... a woman is a universal being. She easily integrates into the culture she marries into and she ensures that her offspring learns the culture.' I consider that statement quite powerful and liberating. Unfortunately, many women are not consciously aware of the force, which is a woman. I think this is the result of the fact that many societies downplay the nurturing and care-giving role of the woman because there are no economic values attached to these roles that appear to be within the exclusive purview of the female.

It is in this nurturing and care-giving role that her evolution is most evident for she sacrifices herself that others may have life. For a greater part of her life, she literally has no identity. As a girl she is someone's daughter and then she evolved into someone's wife and takes on her husband's name and assumes another name, the child's, as she becomes a mother. It is considered a sign of respect in the Yoruba culture to address her as the mother of so and so. Her given name is forgotten and with it her identity as a person in her own right. As she becomes more advanced in age and the physical signs of ageing begin to manifest, she assumes the role of 'mother' of society for everyone refers to her as 'mother'. These changing and evolving roles could be quite daunting at the onset and the adjustment period varies from woman to woman. Unfortunately, some women go through this earthly life without making the needed adjustment into the maturing and matured woman. They could not make the transition from biological to spiritual maturation. Put differently, spiritual maturation did not follow the biological maturation.

The average man was brought up to believe that he is superior to the woman and that she is there to cater to all his whims and caprices. The girl child unconsciously, absorbs this same message and this programming is deeply ingrained in her psyche that she actually feels and thinks herself less than the man, in many respects. She discounts her role in the home and places higher premium on the man's role as provider. Then a time comes in her evolution when she begins to introspect and starts questioning the status quo. Society frowns at this and devices all manner of subterfuge to keep her in check. Her greatest critic, during this phase of her development, the quest for self-expression and self-realization, is her fellow woman. So strong is the opposition that many a woman balked. Those who persisted eventually gained respect and adoration from society.

This quest for self-expression and self-realization becomes heightened with the onset of the 'empty nest' syndrome. This period can be quite daunting and traumatic for many women, who hitherto defined their importance and relevance in life from caring for their husbands and children. The empty nest syndrome brings about a feeling of worthlessness. Fortunately, this is changing. I was quite happy the other day at a Toastmasters' meeting when a young lady gave a speech with the title, 'Remove the Pause'. She lost her husband relatively early in their marriage and she single handedly raised their children. She said that her life had been on hold, a pause, while she was raising them. She joined Toastmasters to get back her voice and take up her life that had been on pause. It was quite a picturesque illustration of the life of an average woman.

When a woman evolves to this stage, she no longer seeks the approbation of others. She goes on stage because that is her choice and she can initiate the applause. She learns to be her own cheerleader and enjoy the hearty approbation of others. Then something happens from within. She realizes for the first time that people had always wanted to assist her along but were only waiting for her to take the lead. She ventures out some more, taking little giant steps until the new woman is born. At that stage, there is no stopping her.

No one can predict the time it will take for the evolutionary process. For some, a major trauma or upheaval will birth the process – the reality of single parenthood, being thrust into a leadership position are some examples. And for others, the change is more gradual and imperceptible. For this second category, they are not aware that an internal change is taking place. A third group are those who work consciously and assiduously to bring it about. Whatever method it takes to bring about this change, society is better for it.

The evolved woman understands who she is and the force that she can bring to bear to change situations and circumstances. It is only from understanding myself that I was able to make the needed change. I started out speaking up and standing by my point of view even against all odds. Throughout my career as a banker, I had only men as my role models. For them too it was strange to have a woman in their cubicle. Many times I was a lone voice. It bothered me and I tried to win others to my side. The more I tried the more I got rejected. Those whose opinions I thought mattered often disappointed me. It did not take me time to realize that many men make decisions from personal biases. A light bulb went on in my head one day and I realized I actually enjoyed being a lone voice. It meant I could occupy the stage alone in full view! What became most pleasing and strengthening was that time proved me right, most times. That realization strengthened me and galvanized me into trying to understand the world of men. I must pay tribute to all those great authors whose works cut short my learning period. They, male and female, were my unknown mentors. The books that had the greatest impact were those insightful ones about what goes on under the glass ceiling, books about office politics. I had naively thought that it was enough to be intelligent and hardworking to get ahead in the office. How wrong I was! The icing on the cake was that I became so skilled in office politics that I introduced it into the organization's learning curriculum to guide the employees, male and female from the land mines. I did not want others, particularly hard working and intelligent ladies, to go through my experience.

I've come to realize that finding one's voice as a woman does not mean one should adopt the seeming bravado style of a man. It is difficult to achieve this balance because there is a dearth of female role models, not because there are no female achievers but because they have been much vilified by society and so the upcoming lady does not want to be associated with her. Fortunately, things are changing for the better.

I would not trade being a woman for all the gold in the world! A woman, who is aware, is powerful beyond measure. There is not a single successful man living, who did not have a female influence to back him up. If it's not his mother, it is a sister, wife or a friend. The story is not exactly the same for the woman. She succeeded, most times, in spite of the man.

Society gains nothing by the weak woman. It is only the strong woman, who is comfortable in her flesh and in her role as a woman, who gives the man permission to be man. Even the institution of marriage thrives on this. If the man is the 'head' of the family, the woman is the neck. A strong neck holds the head better. The evolved woman knows how to lead even from a seeming position of weakness. She stoops to conquer. Men have this mortal fear of women and many men have devised several means to crush women thinking they need to crush her for them to be strong. They mistake physical strength for power. Men who are highly evolved would tell you that a woman's strength lies not in her physique but in her spirit. They will tell you that the woman is spiritually superior to the man.

Ultimately, the desire is for a more enlightened and evolved society. Both man and woman need to be enlightened. A few weeks ago, a septuagenarian male friend, who had been married for 36 years, told me: '... you know, it is only within the last seven years that I've come to realize the importance of woman and her spiritual strength and I started respecting my wife.'

Had the woman been aware of whom she is and her role in the home and society, humanity would have made more progress. Discounting the woman hurts everyone. Since the one who rocks the cradle rules the world, attention should be paid to her formation and education. A self-realized woman liberates the world around her.

'The biological fact of being born a woman is a potential capable of evolving into myriads of possibilities in accordance with the *functions and roles she is called upon to perform in life. She can limit the possibilities based on the thoughts and choices she makes and ultimately her level of consciousness. As her consciousness expands and she becomes more aware of herself and the role of the female in Creation, and makes a conscious choice to cooperate with Nature in that role, Nature will empower her to make manifest her endowment as a woman to help humanity to grow. This is evolution for her and humanity. Individually and collectively, humanity's strive for growth is in an upward spiral. This growth is more spiritual than physical. Since 'no one throws pearls at swine' Nature will only ennoble and empower the evolved woman to carry out this noble role for and on behalf of the Universe. No limitation can therefore be placed on such a woman. She can become anything and everything she wills to become.*

Oladunni Olasehan A retired banker with approximately 26 years of experience; human resources specialist, Oladunni is also a student of philosophy and metaphysics, speaks and writes English and French, edits books, magazines and journals and video recordings. She is a Fashion designer and the Distinguished Toastmasters Award holder - the highest award bestowed by Toastmasters International.

So what is the worth of a woman?

God considers her to be of inestimable value that His Son, Jesus, died for her. Significantly, when Jesus resurrected, it was a woman, Mary, who first saw Him!

'But Mary stood outside by the tomb weeping, and as she wept she stooped down and looked into the tomb. 12 And she saw two angels in white sitting, one at the head and the other at the feet, where the body of Jesus had lain. Then they said to her, "Woman, why are you weeping?" She said to them, "Because they have taken away my Lord, and I do not know where they have laid Him."

"Now when she had said this, she turned around and saw Jesus standing there, and did not know that it was Jesus.

Jesus said to her, "Woman, why are you weeping? Whom are you seeking?" She, supposing Him to be the gardener, said to Him, "Sir, if You have carried Him away, tell me where You have laid Him, and I will take Him away."

Jesus said to her, "Mary!"

She turned and said to Him,[a] "Rabboni!" (which is to say, Teacher).

Jesus said to her, "Do not cling to Me, for I have not yet ascended to My Father; but go to My brethren and say to them, 'I am ascending to My Father and your Father, and to My God and your God.'"

Mary Magdalene came and told the disciples that she had seen the Lord, [b] and that He had spoken these things to her.'

John 20:11-18

Call it 'evolution' or 'self-realization' or 'regeneration', whenever a woman comes to discover, understand and appreciate the purpose of her creation and begins to live accordingly, not only is she fulfilled, humanity benefits tremendously from her self-awareness, and her Maker is glorified.

Part of the objectives of this book would have been accomplished if it helps more women to gain this consciousness and determination to live a purpose- driven life. A virtuous woman, when found, is priceless.

Chapter Three

Who Is A Woman Of Substance?

'Who can find a Virtuous woman? For her prize is far
above rubies'

Proverbs 31:10(NKJV)

There is a deposit, a substance or treasure that distinguishes a woman of substance. She is not a mere woman, she is extraordinary. Humbly conscious of her worth, she carries herself with grace and decorum. Sometimes, she is misunderstood and misrepresented. Some may see her as arrogant because she will not associate with every Tom, Dick, and Harry. She is keenly aware of Who she represents and must represent Him well. What sets a woman of substance apart?

Characteristics of a Woman of Substance

Everything that God created is good. In the Bible, the book of Genesis tells us that,

'Then God saw everything that He had made, and indeed it was very good. So the evening and the morning were the sixth day.'

Genesis 1:31 (NKJV)

However, of all of God's creation, it is only upon the man and the woman that He pronounced His blessings, having created them in His own image.

'Then God said, 'Let Us make man in Our image, according to Our likeness; let them have dominion over the fish of the sea, over the birds of the air, and over the cattle, over all[a] the earth and over every creeping thing that creeps on the earth.' 27 'So God created man in His own image; in the image of God He created him; male and female He created them.' 28 'Then God blessed them, and God said to them, 'Be fruitful and multiply; fill the earth and subdue it; have dominion over the fish of the sea, over the birds of the air, and over every living thing that moves on the earth.'

Genesis 1:26 -28

These creational blessings automatically bestow certain privileges on man. For instance, to a large extent, man shares physical, moral, and intellectual likeness with God.

> *'Out of the ground the Lord God formed every beast of the field and every bird of the air, and brought them to Adam to see what he would call them. And whatever Adam called each living creature, that was its name. So Adam gave names to all cattle, to the birds of the air, and to every beast of the field. But for Adam there was not found a helper comparable to him.'*

Genesis 2:19-20

Man is created with the ability to be holy and righteous,

> *'and that you put on the new man which was created according to God, in true righteousness and holiness.'*

Ephesians 4:24

Man has emotions, mind, and power of choice according to Genesis 2:19-20. And unlike animals, man shares some physical likeness with God. Genesis 18:1-2 says:

> *'Then the Lord appeared to him by the terebinth trees of Mamre,[a] as he was sitting in the tent door in the heat of the day. 2 So he lifted his eyes and looked, and behold, three men were standing by him; and when he saw them, he ran from the tent door to meet them, and bowed himself to the ground.'*

We have an account of how God physically paid His friend, Abraham a visit at which time He promised him a son. This same image was how His Son appeared on earth several years later.

> *'...but made Himself of no reputation, taking the form of a bondservant, and coming in the likeness of men.'*

Philippians 2:7

However, because of sin, man fell and so lost almost all his creational gifts and abilities. But, in Christ Jesus, he is able to recover all.

Accordingly, every woman has value. She is gifted, talented and endowed with strength, wisdom, and knowledge to discover and fulfill the purpose of her creation. Ample opportunities are also provided for her to express her uniqueness and gifting.

But, do all women get to discover and fulfill their purpose? A Bible story exemplifies the point being made here. It is the story of Daniel, and his three friends at Babylon where the king compelled them all to eat his special delicacy but Daniel alone purposed in his mind that he was not going to defile himself with the king's delicacy. Evidently, others ate the king's delicacy because we never read about them any longer. Only Daniel made history! Why? Because he knew his purpose and determined in his heart that nothing was going to rob him of the fulfillment of that purpose. In like manner, a woman of substance makes history. She exemplifies certain characteristics which are discussed below. These characteristics are in no way exhaustive.

1). **Right Priorities:** Being a woman of substance starts with giving priority to the right things.

She recognizes and makes God her number one priority. Nourishing her relationship with God, she sees value in herself and is determined to be worthy of honor and commendation. This means that as a woman, you understand that you are not just a number, you have value and you have a place in God's eternal plan. Mordecai, Esther's uncle reminded her that the purpose of her being a queen transcended the perquisites of her position as Queen. She was reminded that her purpose was higher. Thankfully, she yielded, had a rethink and eventually fulfilled her divine purpose of saving her nation from being completely annihilated.

Some women fail to recognize their relevance outside of their husbands, if they are married. If they are not married, what gives them relevance is the value and amount of jewelry they possess or their beauty and sometimes, their father's riches or career. All those things are temporal and cannot endure pains, trials, and challenges of life when they come – for they will surely come. Woman, who or what is your priority?

2). **Self-secure**: A woman of substance is a confident woman.
She is secure in who she is and does not want to be like anyone else. Even though she admires good qualities in others, she neither compares herself with them nor wants to be like them.

'For we dare not class ourselves or compare ourselves with those who commend themselves. But they, measuring themselves by themselves, and comparing themselves among themselves, are not wise.'

2 Corinthians 10:12.

Do not compare yourself with others. Mary is content to be at Jesus' feet, learning and soaking in the word of life. She is not intimidated by her sister, Martha's constant chides to help with guests' entertainment.

> *'And she had a sister called Mary, who also sat at Jesus' feet and heard His word. 40 But Martha was distracted with much serving, and she approached Him and said, 'Lord, do You not care that my sister has left me to serve alone? Therefore tell her to help me.' And Jesus[l] answered and said to her, 'Martha, Martha, you are worried and troubled about many things. 42 But one thing is needed, and Mary has chosen that good part, which will not be taken away from her.'*

Luke 10:39-42

3) **Purpose:** A woman of substance is purpose-driven.
Her convictions are God-centered and derived from what she knows to be the plans and purpose of God for her life. Because God is the Giver of life, He determines the purpose of the life created.

> *'For I know the thoughts that I think toward you, says the Lord, thoughts of peace and not of evil, to give you a future and a hope.'*

Jeremiah 29:11.

Purpose is revealed and discovered as you get intimate with God in prayer, in worship, and as you study and meditate on His word.

> *'Now acquaint yourself with Him, and be at peace; There by good will come to you.'*
>
> *Job 22:21.*

As you get intimate with God, He will start to place burdens in your heart. Burdens that weigh heavily upon the heart sooner or later become our life purpose. Deborah said her heart was with the rulers of Israel. That means her thoughts often trailed to Israel rulers, she cared about their well-being. What gave them horrors were of concern to her. She cared deeply for them. Therefore, when the opportunity arose for her to save her national leaders from the enemies' embarrassment and harassment, even when it meant going to the battle field, Deborah was highly motivated to do so!

Many people are living life without a purpose. Our Creator is purposeful in all He does. He has plans and purpose for you; you must discover it. What are your burdens? What are your concerns? What keeps you awake at night? What do you find yourself often thinking, talking and praying about? What gets you fired up or excited each time a discussion comes up in regards to the subject? Whatever that is might be your purpose. It may not be spiritual. For instance, some people cannot have enough of a discussion that revolves around basketball games. They get excited, their eyes light up anytime a discussion comes up on the game or it is being shown on the TV. That could be an indication that such a fellow might become a world renowned basketball player or coach.

Once your passion is known, prayerfully determine what your personal contribution in life will be; and that in turn becomes the value that drives your convictions. God has invested so much in you; your life must not be wasted. What is your life purpose?

As a trainer and conference speaker, I travel frequently. Although seasonal, so much is the frequency of my travels sometimes that some concerned friends have counseled, especially a few years back, when my two of my children were younger that I should wait at home, take care of my family before going to minister outside. Well, as a minister don't I know that? Don't I teach it? After all that is what is 'expected' of a married woman to do. But you see, I am privileged to have a personal relationship with my Heavenly Father, and daily, I strive to grow in my intimacy with Him such that I allow Him to lead and direct my ways. Therefore, if He has granted me permission to go and minister to His people, and my husband is in support, who's other's permission do I need? This is to say that as a woman of substance, you must be in a right, thriving relationship with God through Jesus, the Access to Him, and be determined to do His will even when you are being misunderstood. Not only that, you must be passionate about your purpose because your passion fuels your purpose.

4) **Focus:** A woman of substance is focused.

It is a known fact that women possess a God-given capability to multi-task. Unlike men, women are naturally talented to coordinate three or more activities at the same time. A woman can be cooking, nursing her baby, answering the phone and doing laundry all at the same time! Even in the midst of competing activities demanding attention, a woman of substance must determine her priorities and order them accordingly. Her goal is not just to be efficient, but she must aim at effectiveness in whatever she does. Jesus Christ observed and commended Mary for discovering and focusing on 'one thing' that is needed and good and which cannot be taken away from her. Her sister, Martha on the other hand was chided for being distracted by too many activities. Are you a Mary or a Martha? Of course, our focus changes per time and season. Not only must you correctly discern the season of your life, you must equally determine what requires your full focus at a given season of your life.

What are you focusing on?

5) **Influence:** A woman of substance wields positive influence.

Women are natural influencers. Our physique, beauty, and charm, if put to good use, can influence decisions that could make or mar families, organizations, churches, nations, and destinies. Eve influenced Adam to eat the forbidden fruit (Gen.2:6).That singular act introduced suspicion into the male/female relationship which God intended to be of mutual benefit. What about Delilah? She deployed her charm and beauty to lure her husband, Samson to divulge a secret he was meant to keep. Have you considered the main reason for Vashti's dethronement?

> *'And Memucan answered before the king and the princes: 'Queen Vashti has not only wronged the king, but also all the princes, and all the people who are in all the provinces of King Ahasuerus. 17 For the queen's behavior will become known to all women, so that they will despise their husbands in their eyes, when they report, 'King Ahasuerus commanded Queen Vashti to be brought in before him, but she did not come.' 18 This very day the noble ladies of Persia and Media will say to all the king's officials that they have heard of the behavior of the queen. Thus there will be excessive contempt and wrath. 19 If it pleases the king, let a royal decree go out from*

him, and let it be recorded in the laws of the Persians and the Medes, so that it will not be altered, that Vashti shall come no more before King Ahasuerus; and let the king give her royal position to another who is better than she. 20. When the king's decree which he will make is proclaimed throughout all his empire (for it is great), all wives will honor their husbands, both great and small.'

Esther 1:16-20

Queen Vashti was dethroned because of the fear that her refusal to appear before her husband, the king, will negatively impact other women to disrespect their husbands! Esther, on the other hand, used her position as Queen to influence a decision that benefitted her people. Deborah used her calling, talent, and gift to bring victory to her nation by supporting Barak, the Captain of Israel army. In contemporary times, we have had women like Mother Theresa, Olufunmilayo Ransome-Kuti, Mariam Babangida, Michelle Obama, Pastor Folu Adeboye and others who used their positions to positively impact their spheres of influence.

God has positioned women strategically as 'help meet'. Whether as wives, mothers, professional colleagues, sisters, pastors or politicians, women are endowed with natural and spiritual gifts that could impact their spheres of influence positively, if discovered. As a woman, you must constantly expose yourself to the needs around you and seek to meet them. You have what it takes! What are the needs are you meeting where you are located? How are you influencing those around you?

6) **Fear of God:** A woman of substance is God fearing.

It is a fear that is borne out of intimate and correct knowledge of who God is. It is not a fearful fear. It is a fear that reckons with the attributes that make God who He is and makes one want to emulate Him. A woman can be good without being Godly but it is impossible to be a Godly woman without being good. Are you just good but ungodly? Godliness is Christ-likeness and vice versa. Jesus is the Way to live Godly, the Truth about Godliness and the Life of Godliness. In Him, we live, we move and have our being; He is **'the true Light which gives light to every man who comes into the world.'** (John 1:9).

The Proverbs 31 woman is a woman of exemplary character, strength, and ability. It is instructive to note that despite all the accolades poured on this woman, reference was not made to her physical appearance. Instead, her fear of God appears to be the dominating factor for her distinctiveness. '**Charm is deceitful and beauty is passing, but a woman who fears**

the Lord, she shall be praised.' (Prov. 31: 30). Are you a good woman or a Godly woman? Do you fear God?

On a scale of 1 - 10, where do you rate your intimacy with God? A woman of substance is not just a number; she adds value to her world – family, community, place of work, all her social and religious contacts. Here's what a young lady I call Ms. M has to say.

> *'The whole world stood to honor Barack & Michelle Obama yesterday...were they not ever gorgeous! Some spouse adds value, yes, Barack is the President of the United States of America, but do you see how much substance Michelle has in herself? It has nothing to do with the office they occupy, her CV shows how solid she is...her office comes with glamour and fashion but those things do not make her. Her quality enhances her beauty. As a woman, a man should specially thank God for adding you to his life! Is your value only about your shoes, make up and bags? When you increase your love for God and seek after Him, He adds value that money cannot buy to you. While your husband may not be a President of a nation, he is the president of your home. Ensure you add value to his life!'*

7) **A woman of substance reproduces herself.**
Because she is humbly conscious of the 'treasure' within her, she strives to disciple, mentor or coach her likes who will carry on her legacies after she's gone. Jesus Christ did exactly

just that. Through His exemplary life and teachings, Jesus mentored his disciples and commanded them to go and do similarly,

> *'Go therefore and make disciples of all nations, baptizing them in the name of the Father and of the Son and of the Holy Spirit, teaching them to observe all things that I have commanded you; and lo I am with you always, even to the end of the age.'*

Matthew 28:19-20

As I write this bit, I am reminded of an incident that happened in my church in 2008. We were rounding up our Women Conference (which had commenced a few days earlier) at our Sunday Worship Service. As is customary, the officiating women gathered to pray before taking their seats with me presiding as Pastor's wife. As I was about to assign functions that each person would perform, the Spirit of God spoke to my heart to me that I should ask one of our young female adults to open the service with what we call 'Congregational Prayer'. That was absurd because 'normally' a woman should perform that function; after all it was a women event. Nonetheless, I mentioned it to my husband and he merely asked me to go ahead since the Spirit spoke to my heart. I did. It was unbelievable what those ten-minutes 'prayer session' turned out to be – a fervent cry, better described as groaning in the spirit for help and guidance from 'mothers in the house' as she put it. She cried, 'mothers we need you!' I was visibly shaken and I knew there and then that the Lord was chastening older women in the church for lacking in their duties of mentoring younger females in the church. My mind went to the Book of Titus in the Bible:

3 Bid the older women similarly to be reverent and devout in their deportment as becomes those engaged in sacred service, not slanderers or slaves to drink. They are to give good counsel and be teachers of what is right and noble,

4 So that they will wisely train the young women to be [a] sane and sober of mind (temperate, disciplined) and to love their husbands and their children,

5 To be self-controlled, chaste, homemakers, good-natured (kindhearted), adapting and subordinating themselves to their husbands, that the word of God may not be exposed to reproach (blasphemed or discredited).

6 In a similar way, urge the younger men to be self-restrained and to behave prudently [taking life seriously].

7 And show your own self in all respects to be a pattern and a model of good deeds and works, teaching what is unadulterated, showing gravity [having the

**strictest regard for truth and purity of motive], with
dignity and seriousness.'**

Titus 2:3-7

Amplified Bible (AMP)

After that Conference, we started a Fellowship for young
female adults in the church called 'Esther's Fellowship.' It is
through this medium that the older women are mentoring,
coaching and providing the needed guidance for this group of
young ladies who are so vulnerable to worldly influences that
could truncate their destinies if timely care is not taken.

A good man, (and women too) leaves an inheritance for their
children,

**'A good man leaves an inheritance to his children's
children, But the wealth of the sinner is stored up for the
righteous.'**

Proverbs 13:22

8) **Teachability** is an essential character quality of a
Woman of Substance. Teachability says, 'I am open to
correction, I am amenable to discipline because I know
it is for my good.' This trait is lacking in many today
unfortunately. I am reminded of my younger days as
an Executive Officer in Human Resources
Department, Afribank Nigeria Plc. I worked with a

dynamic woman, self-assured, diligent, who spoke the English Language impeccably. I had a lot of respect for and submitted to her leadership even though at a point we were both Departmental heads in our own rights. I would take my draft memos to her for correction. Mrs. O. as I fondly call her would 'pieces' my write up with her red ink pen, write comments and say to me, 'your write ups are too wordy, learn to write compact sentences, most people, especially executives don't have time to read lengthy memos!' Sometimes, I rewrite a memo three times before Mrs.O will okay my write-up. That was part of my tutelage growing up. That in part shaped who I am today. I tried her system with an intern who worked with me in the same establishment; she rebuffed my 'arrogance!' A woman that will distinguish herself from others must humbly submit to a higher authority.

In conclusion, let no one, woman or man, be intimidated by the picture painted here of a woman of substance. Like the Proverbs 31 woman, you grow into this image. Luke 2:52 states, "Jesus increased in wisdom, knowledge, and understanding', indicating that a woman of substance is that powerful, self-secure, God-focused individual that you can progressively become. Becoming a woman of substance does not happen overnight, you have to build-up to it. This book gives practical steps to becoming that phenomenal woman of substance, and provides reflection from women who are a living proof. Learn from women that came before you, listen to their stories and learn from their mistakes. Rather than envy, emulate the God-given qualities in the lives of others around you. Do not be intimated by it, desire to be one; and God will teach you Himself.

Chapter Four

The Purpose of a Woman

'For I know the thoughts that I think toward you, says the Lord, thoughts of peace and not of evil, to give you a future and a hope.'

Jeremiah 29:11 (NKJV)

Numerous controversies revolve around the purpose, role, rights and the place of the woman, even in the twenty-first century! At the center of these controversies is the woman herself. Although the situation is improving, many women still have identity crisis. Some women are still struggling to discover as well as to understand who they are, their purpose, relevance and place in the family, workplace, community, and the world.

Dr. Myles Munroe in his book, *UNDERSTANDING THE PURPOSE AND POWER OF WOMAN* wrote, '**Women of every culture and society are facing the dilemma of identity. Traditional views of what it means to be a**

**woman and changing cultural and marital roles are
causing women conflict in their relationship with men.
Women are under tremendous stress as they struggle to
discover who they are and what role they are to play
today – in the family, the community, and the world.'**

For women to be secure and live a fulfilled life devoid of any
anxieties relating to their gender, they need to know the
purpose of their existence. Everything in life is created for a
purpose. Purpose is the reason for which something exists or
is done, made or used. It also refers to an intended or desired
result; an aim or goal. When the purpose or intent of
something is not known, that thing is subject to abuse or
misuse. The appropriate person who can correctly spell out
the purpose of an object is the maker or designer of that
object. Therefore, God being the creator of mankind is the
best person to tell us the purpose for which He created a
woman!

The purpose of God and man do not always align. What we
as humans consider good may be evil in the sight of God and
sometimes what we disregard as unworthy is what God
elevates. The story in the Bible of how David was anointed
king over the nation of Israel is a good example. In 1 Samuel
16:4-13, we read. . . **'So Samuel did what the Lord said,
and went to Bethlehem. And the elders of the town
trembled at his coming, and said, "Do you come**

peaceably?" And he said, "Peaceably; I have come to sacrifice to the Lord. Sanctify yourselves, and come with me to the sacrifice." Then he consecrated Jesse and his sons, and invited them to the sacrifice. So it was, when they came, that he looked at Eliab and said, "Surely the Lord's anointed is before Him!" But the Lord said to Samuel, "Do not look at his appearance or at his physical stature, because I have refused him. For the Lord does not see as man sees;[a] for man looks at the outward appearance, but the Lord looks at the heart." So Jesse called Abinadab, and made him pass before Samuel. And he said, "Neither has the Lord chosen this one." Then Jesse made Shammah pass by. And he said, "Neither has the Lord chosen this one." 10 Thus Jesse made seven of his sons pass before Samuel. And Samuel said to Jesse, "The Lord has not chosen these." 11 And Samuel said to Jesse, "Are all the young men here?" Then he said, "There remains yet the youngest, and there he is, keeping the sheep." And Samuel said to Jesse, "Send and bring him. For we will not sit down[b] till he comes here." 12 So he sent and brought him in. Now he was ruddy, with bright eyes, and good-looking. And the Lord said, "Arise, anoint him; for this is the one!" 13 Then Samuel took the horn of oil and anointed him in the midst of his brothers; and the Spirit of the Lord came upon David from that day forward. So Samuel arose and went to Ramah.'

Dr. Myles Munroe puts it this way, "we have many plans, but God has a purpose" and almost always, God's plans must prevail if we want to be successful and happy in life.

'Many are the plans in a man's heart, but it is the Lord's purpose that prevails.'

Proverbs 19:21

Many women are living a frustrated, unfulfilled life today because they are either too busy trying to be like another woman, have too many commitments or little time to clearly discern God's plan for their life. Some women on the other hand have not understood the wisdom in living a purposeful life. Do you reading this book fall into any of these categories? I am glad to inform you that you are not alone! Just read on, you will find the help that you need in order to overcome your challenge.

So what was the plan and purpose of God in creation for man? The first thing we know is that because God is good, He certainly created a woman for a good purpose. God is intentional in all He does. He has a plan and a purpose for everything and everyone, including you!

His purpose for creating the woman is clearly stated in His manual for anyone who cares to read. . .

[18]'Now the Lord God said, It is not good (sufficient, satisfactory) that the man should be alone; I will make him a helper (suitable, adapted, complementary) for him.

[19] And out of the ground the Lord God formed every [wild] beast and living creature of the field and every bird of the air and brought them to Adam to see what he would call them; and whatever Adam called every living creature, that was its name.

[20] And Adam gave names to all the livestock and to the birds of the air and to every [wild] beast of the field; but for Adam there was not found a helper meet (suitable, adapted, complementary) for him.

[21] And the Lord God caused a deep sleep to fall upon Adam; and while he slept, He took one of his ribs or a part of his side and closed up the [place with] flesh.'

Genesis 2:18-21
Amplified Bible (AMP)

The woman must understand that she is an essential, irreplaceable, significant entity in creation; an integral part of God's creation plan. You are not an afterthought. The woman created by God is meant to be a suitable, needed, comparable companion for the man. Equal before God, both the man and the woman have complementary roles to play which are mutually exclusive. When a woman understands that as a 'helper', she procreates, nurses, counsels, comforts, nurtures, encourages, uplifts, reasons, delivers and does so many other things which our 'Divine Helper' does especially if she is in a right relationship with God, she is fulfilled.

In this unique position, she is already validated by God as an able, capable human being and so does not need the validation of anyone else. Because the society has defined the woman differently from how her Creator intended her to be, which has left many women insecure, abused and misused, women need to reconnect with God through His Word, and believe who He says they are. When this happens, women will live purposefully and will be respected better than they are right now. As author Myles Munroe rightly says, 'a woman cannot fulfill her purpose unless she is in a relationship with God.'

Chapter Five

To My Single Sisters, I Write. . .

'The horse is prepared for the day of battle, But, deliverance is of the LORD.'

Proverbs 21:31(NKJV)

By the time a lady attains a certain age, depending on the culture she belongs to; she begins to nurse the idea of settling down in marriage. In the African culture that I am familiar with, an educated lady will begin to experience some level of pressure from family and friends by age 25 to 29 if she is not in a relationship that everyone expects to end in marriage.

I got married at the age of 29, almost 30, therefore I am writing from experience! At a point, my family members, meaning well, were saying to me, 'What else do you want? You have a Master's degree, you have a nice car, and you have a good job. . .' As if those are all that one needs in order to get married and build a home! With benefits of hindsight, I wish to counsel single ladies and young men as well that marriage is very good, because God ordained it. But it is only good when done according to His ways. Do not allow anyone to pressurize, seduce, or lure you into marriage!

A lot of preparations are needful in order to build a good marriage. Spiritual, emotional, physical, psychological, mental, and financial preparations are expedient.

The experience of Esther, in the Book of Esther is very instructive in this regard. There is a biblical account of a king Ahasuerus, who, after an unusual one hundred and eighty days of partying, displaying the riches and splendor of his kingdom, commanded his queen to come and show off her beauty to his people and officials. The queen, Vashti declined and the king, feeling humiliated, became furious. To pacify him, his counselors advised that Queen Vashti be dethroned and replaced with a better lady.

> *'Then the king's servants who attended him said: 'Let beautiful young virgins be sought for the king; and let the king appoint officers in all the provinces of his kingdom, that they may gather all the beautiful young virgins to Shushan the citadel, into the women's quarters, under the custody of Hega[a] the king's eunuch, custodian of the women. And let beauty preparations be given them.[4] Then let the young woman who pleases*

the king be queen instead of Vashti. This thing pleased the king, and he did so.'

Esther 2:2-4

Esther, an orphan, being raised by an uncle named Mordecai, was enrolled as a possible queen for the king. It is recorded that Esther, like all other likely candidates, went through *one year beauty preparations* before appearing before the king so he could assess them and decide if they met his expectations!

'Each young woman's turn came to go in to king Ahasuerus after she had completed twelve months' preparation, according to the regulations for the women, for thus were the days of their preparation apportioned: six months with oil of myrrh, and six months with perfumes and preparations for beautifying women. [13] Thus prepared, each young woman went to the king, and she was given whatever she desired to take with her from the women's quarters to the king's palace.'

Esther 2:12-13

After completing twelve months preparation, Esther was presented to the King and

63

> *'the king loved Esther more than all the other women. . . . Then the King made a great feast, the Feast of Esther, for all his officials and servants and proclaimed a holiday in the provinces and gave gifts according to the generosity of a king.'*

Esther 2: 17 -18

Single ladies, your preparation before marriage will determine how successful your marriage is and how happy you are in it. This is the time of your preparation. The starting point in your preparation is to know yourself. You need to reflect on who you are. Ask yourself these questions: Who am I? What are my likes and dislikes? What type of personality do I have? What is my temperament like? If you do not know yourself, it gets very challenging getting to know or understand your partner.

You must address your mind to the following questions:

- Besides your beauty, good academic performance and possibly a good, well-paying job, what other values are you adding to your relationship? Those things listed above are very essential but unfortunately they don't keep your home, at least for long.

- What are your values? What are your personal ethics? What are those things you value so much you cannot compromise? Do you value good character? Do you find bad attitudes offensive? Do you have one? Are you easily irritated?

- What are your moral standards? Do you care about integrity? Can you take it if you are cheated?

- Suppose what you desire most in a relationship is not easily forthcoming, how long can you endure?

- Are you a good cook? Most men appreciate good food! Queen Esther seemed to understand this – in order to get the attention of her husband the king so she can have her request, she prepared a special banquet twice to which she invited the king before putting forth her request. If you are limited in this area, this is the time to learn.

- Have you thought about your relationship with your future in-laws? Are you a people person? Do you need to work on your interpersonal relations? Do you need to develop skills in people management? In most African cultures, when a woman marries, she is considered married to the entire family, therefore, a woman must be courteous towards her in-laws and learn to accommodate them in her home.

- Do you require some improvement in your attitudes?

- Would you consider working with a Life Coach who can work you through some of your 'issues'? A Life Coach can help to clarify your thoughts and purposes and help you in this transition.

- What about your spiritual standing? Are you standing or rising and falling? Are you in church just to 'catch' a good husband? I tell the young ladies I counsel that it will be unfair of God to give a good man to a bad woman. Usually, you attract your like. Do you possess the qualities you desire in a man? Are you prayerful? Do you delight in God's word, daily meditating in it and allowing it to transform you?

Psalm 119:9 states: **'How can a young man (woman) cleanse his way? By taking heed according to your word.'**

My young ladies, all these are important areas you must focus on before marriage if you are planning to be married and stay married. Also, read the book of Esther and research into the Proverbs 31 woman. You will discover the 'substance' in Esther earned her the favor she received from the king and because she realized that her purpose transcends palatial perquisites, she rose up to the need of her nation and fulfilled destiny by using her influence and position as Queen to bring deliverance to her Jewish nation.

I sought for the counsel of different married women with diverse backgrounds, ages, groups, and professions to young female adults contemplating marriage. Here are some of their responses:

For a young woman growing up, my counsel is that she should first and foremost develop a relationship with Christ, because this lays the foundation as to not only how God sees her, but also, how she should view herself. A young woman must learn to be confident in who she is as a person. This will enable her to develop and understand her own self -worth as a woman, and ultimately this will translate into how she takes care of herself physically, emotionally, and spiritually. Her relationship with God will also enable her to guard her heart against things that could easily distract and take her away from her goals and plans she might have for her future. She should be willing to listen, be teachable, and take heed to advice when it is given, especially from other Christian women who have had some experiences in life. My recommendation here is that she seeks mentors from varied backgrounds in life. These would be women whom she admires, respects, and have some level of influence. A young woman must also realize that she will have some failures in life, but the true test is whether she learns from it and move on. Through it all she should understand that she is not a failure. Last, I would say young women must learn to develop broad and diverse interests, hobbies and activities as this makes her a well- rounded, total person.

(Pastor Manita Fadele is a Medical Doctor specializing in Pediatrics. She is also a pastor and a pastor's wife. She is married to the Chairman RCCGNA, Pastor James Fadele. They have been happily married for 24 years.)

Here's another counsel, from a younger sister who has been happily married to the same husband for 11 years. I call her Ms. M- she has a ministry named DIVINE POSSIBILITIES on Facebook which focuses on building, restoring, and encouraging Godly marital relationships:

So by now, you know I don't just get a kick from hanging out with singles. I am on a mission by the grace of God. Being single is not a crime or weakness; it is just a training period, a period where you prepare for the journey of marriage by learning from examples around us. There are positive as well as negative lessons all around, when you are not in the shoes of those affected, judgment is usually fierce. God expects you to pick out danger signals when you discover what tripped your peer. Are you already planning a wedding? What are your priorities? Are you one of those who think it must be a high class wedding ceremony or none at all.

I recall the simplicity involved in planning a wedding a few years ago, thank God for event planners and all the sites that can make you feel like getting married all over again because of the glamorous and exquisite decorations and effects. I love attending weddings and am trusting God for a few this year by His mercies...but a question that I cannot stop pondering about in my mind is why do people inconvenience themselves for what they cannot afford? The fact that someone had a society wedding where roads were closed, endless number of color matching, color blocking, feeding, and what have you took place should not make you go beyond your means. The work in marriage has nothing to do with the work that you put into the coordination of your wedding. Real work starts when you begin to live with your spouse and you discover who they really are and the effort that you have to put in to make your homework. The bible calls it home building...Proverbs 14:1 'every wise woman builds her home, but the foolish plucks it down with her hands.' It is a walk and work of faith! When the blings and glitz are all done away with, reality sets in, you are forced to ask some questions you failed to ask before. Then it might be a little late, the make-up artist would have collected his/her money, the caterers, musician, organizer and every other business contact would have made their money and be long gone. Then you have to face the reality; outstanding loans to pay, bills to settle, the disappointment of failed promises and so on. There will always be people who are better than us, possess better things, jobs and so on. The essence of who you really are is in accepting yourself and being proud of your achievements no matter how little they seem. The most expensive weddings are not the happiest marriages. Fairytale weddings are good, talk of the town and so on, but know why you want to do what you want to do. Peer pressure can cause permanent damages in some areas. Plan with what you have, let promises be extra, do not base your hopes on promises that can fail you on your most important day! For every one of you getting married soon, I wish you marital bliss!

Being single affords you time for everything; God, work, friends, self and preparation for a godly home if you so desire. Preparation precedes promotion, if you fail to prepare for your place of promotion, you may find yourself becoming miserable or ridiculed. Marriage requires a lot of work that is why you cannot afford to allow yourself to be coerced, talked or lured into it. All your senses have to be at work and you must know for a fact that you are being led into a relationship by the spirit of God.

Preparing for marriage entails bringing value, whether you are a man or woman, you must be adding value to your relationship. Once the euphoria of the passive state of falling in love is gone, your real picture is revealed. You do not have to pattern your relationship after anyone else's because your team (you and spouse) are different. You have to agree on what works for you and that will be subject to continuous review as you mature. For everyone who desires to build a godly home, there is a cost to it. A godly home costs virtues; selflessness, prayerfulness, generosity, self-sacrifice, self-denial, courage and of course, love.

Marital love is constantly subjected to tests; that is why you need to be doubly sure that your love has the stamina to stand in the face of challenges. Many relationships these days are born out of selfishness and what the other party has to offer. Try and build a relationship based on God's kind of love so it can stand when the test comes because it is a matter of time, every relationship will be tested for substance (Matthew 7:24-27).

No marriage relationship is promised immunity against tests, so be prepared! Before you can understand your spouse well, you need to *understand yourself. When you know who you are, you have a better perspective of who the other party is. Your personality, temperament, likes, dislikes, all create a window for you to have a clear view of who you are and who your spouse is. Objectivity leaves room for others to make mistakes as well as be who they need to be. Your spouse will be different from you because you were raised differently. 'When you understand that, you do not expect him/her to reason or react the exact way you do.'*

Omolara Ishola is a Registered Nurse She has a blog DIVINE POSSIBILITIES which she frequently shares on FaceBook.

How about getting you a mentor? Esther had a mentor in Mordecai, a well-principled Godly man who successfully coached, guided and instilled in Esther some life lessons that enabled her have a successful marriage as well as fulfill her life purpose. There may not be too many but there are still some good role models – Godly couples who have lived happily together following Biblical principles on marriage. You can prayerfully look for one. The Bible states that

'*Where there is no counsel, the people fall; but in the multitude of counselors there is safety.*'

Proverbs 11:14

Chapter Six

The Journey To Greatness

'Then God said, 'Let Us make man in Our image, according to Our likeness; let them have dominion over the fish of the sea, over the birds of the air, and over the cattle, over all [a] the earth and over every creeping thing that creeps on the earth.' 27 So God created man in His own image; in the image of God He created him; male and female He created them. 28 Then God blessed them, and God said to them, 'Be fruitful and multiply; fill the earth and subdue it; have dominion over the fish of the sea, over the birds of the air, and over every living thing that moves on the earth.'

Genesis 1:26-28 (NKJV)

Every man is born with the seed of greatness in him. Every man is born with the potential to be great. A great God created man; He could not have created a mediocre entity, being a great God Himself. ***Then God said, 'Let Us make man in Our image, according to Our likeness; let them***

have dominion over the fish of the sea, over the birds of the air, and over the cattle, over all [a] the earth and over every creeping thing that creeps on the earth.' (Genesis1:26)

However, not every man becomes great. So what makes some people great, while others do not attain their potential for greatness? The answer to that lies in the fact that greatness is a journey of a lifetime. It is an individualized journey that starts with self-evaluation, leading to self-transformation as you progressively engage in self-development. According to poet- philosopher Noah BerShea, 'greatness isn't ahead of you, it is within you and things don't have to be good for us to be great. Besides, you define what constitutes greatness according to you and you determine how, when and if you want to attain greatness. However, greatness is in you!'

Jesus Christ lent a voice to a universal and timeless teaching similar to what Noah BerShea wrote in his book. He was asked when the kingdom of God would come. Jesus replied, that the kingdom of God is not something people would be able to see and point to, **'nor will they say *"See here!"* or *"See there!"[a] For indeed, the kingdom of God is within you.' (Luke 17:21,)*** In other words, life's ultimate truth, its ultimate treasure, or greatness or success lies within each of us.

If greatness lies within us, how can we bring it to the surface? How can it become a reality? Greatness becomes a reality when you commence a journey of life that starts with 'self-reflection' – Who am I? Where did I come from? Why am I here? What is my life's purpose? How do I accomplish it? You're most likely not going to receive the answers to these questions over-night. Answers will come as you navigate through diverse life experiences; good and bad. And as you persevere, diligently seeking for answers, the answers will come slowly but certainly. If a journey is the act of travelling from one place to another, then attaining greatness starts from a point. A Chinese proverb says 'to get through the hardest journey we need to take only one step at a time, but we must keep on stepping.'

Therefore, in your journey towards greatness, as a woman of substance, understand the following:

1.   Your journey towards greatness, which is the culmination of your self-worth, or value, starts with the dissatisfaction of the status quo. Something in you is being repelled by what is around you that are not in alignment with what is within you. There is a hunger, a search for more. You should be telling yourself 'there should be more to life than this'. Mike Murdock said, 'Intolerance of your present creates your future'. For as long as you can live with or

excuse your present situation, you will never change neither will you be able to attain greatness.

2.   The feeling of dissatisfaction will lead to a search for relevance, truth, something to live for, something you are willing to die for. This search may take different people to different activities, some physical, and some spiritual. Because man is a spiritual being, we often find the answers to our search through our religious beliefs. Jesus Christ told us what we need to seek first in Matthew 6:33 **'But seek first the kingdom of God and His righteousness, and all these things shall be added to you.'** Also, In Luke 10:41-42, Jesus said to Martha, after she had complained to Him about her sister's lack of assistance in serving Him. **'Martha, Martha, you are worried and troubled about many things. 42 But one thing is needed, and Mary has chosen that good part, which will not be taken away from her.'**

Anyone on a journey to greatness must clearly identify and focus on one thing that is most important. That 'one thing' is Jesus. He is the *way* to greatness, the *truth,* about greatness, and, the *life* of greatness. Many people are encumbered with many things. Many care so much about material things at the expense of the Real Thing. Cares of life, making many to engage in a rat race, does not give them the time needed to spend in solitude, and in the self – retrospection that will lead them to the detection of their life's purpose. *'You will show me the path of life,; In Your presence is fullness of joy; at you right hand pleasures forevermore' (Psalm 16:11).* *'Seeking to know your life purpose requires diligence and persistence. God said in the Bible,' Jeremiah 29:13, 'You will seek me and find me when you search for me with all your heart.'*

3. To be great, you must have visions, and your vision must be clear. It is difficult to get to a place that you cannot see. Therefore, you must have a mental picture of your preferred future – that is what vision is. *'Write the vision, and make it plain on tablets, that he may run who reads it.' (Habakkuk2:2)* You must see your vision, dream about it, talk about it, write it down and share it.

4.   On your journey towards greatness, you must be willing to take risks. Harry Gray once said, 'No one ever achieved greatness by playing it safe.' Many great people we read about defied the odds that were against them and turned those odds into great inventions. For instance, Benjamin Franklin put his life at risk in his attempts to decrease the amount of fires started by lightning; he created the lightning rod. So also, Thomas Edison improved the light bulb by making it more practical and useful.

Jesus was a risk taker. He was unconventional in his teaching and approach. Contrary to the cultural beliefs of His time, for someone who claimed to be the Messiah, He dined and wined with sinners, related freely with women, and boldly condemned the religious leaders of the time for their hypocrisies.

5. Greatness comes through service. Thomas Edison and Benjamin Franklin saw a need and sought to fill such needs. Often times, they recognized that someone needed help and they provided such help. In a similar way, Jesus came to serve humanity. He said to his disciples in **Matthew 20:26-27, '*Yet it shall not be so among you; but whoever desires to become great among you, let him be your servant. And whoever desires to be first among you, let him be your slave*'.**

Countless opportunities to serve abound all around us and we are all well gifted to meet such needs. You can become great in your gifts. There are people seeking for wise counsel, direction, and guidance, others need comfort and encouragement. If you are gifted in one of those areas, then provide the service! '*Having then gifts differing according to the grace that is given to us, let us use them: if prophecy, let us prophesy in proportion to our faith; 7 or ministry, let us use it in our ministering; he who teaches, in teaching;' (Romans 12:6-7)*

6. Great people are influencers; they are leaders. They lead others towards a cause they believe in. As leaders, they are people of good character. They value virtues like love, integrity, kindness, humility, compassion, diligence, and courage. Great people abhor hypocritical tendencies; they are true to themselves and to people around them. Jesus Christ rebuked the Pharisees of his time saying, *'Woe to you, scribes and Pharisees, hypocrites! For you pay tithe of mint and anise and cummin, and have neglected the weightier matters of the law: justice and mercy and faith. These you ought to have done, without leaving the others undone.' (Matthew 23:23)*

7. Great people are disciplined people. Cultivate disciplined habits, like regular studying, healthy eating, regular saving, giving, and fasting, and you will find yourself attaining greatness little by little. Discipline is defined as 'training that leads to correction or molding of character or perfection. It is control gained by obedience or development through instruction and exercise especially in self-control.' Jesus Christ modeled discipline in His habits. He habitually isolated Himself to re-energize and re-focus. He went to solitary places to pray. His

disciplined prayer life was so impressive, His disciples asked Him to teach them how to pray.

8.   And finally, you must have faith. To have faith is to believe first in yourself, next in dreams (that you are are able to accomplish your goal), and finally believe in God. As Henry Ford once said, 'Whether you think you can, or whether you think you can't, you're right.' You will succeed in life to the extent of the confidence you have in yourself. However, that is not enough. Your confidence in God for ability, divine help and unmerited favor will go a long way in your journey towards greatness in life. God has pre-determined your greatness, and you will do well to go to Him to discover His plans for you and how to accomplish it. God said, **'For I know the thoughts that I think toward you, says the Lord, thoughts of peace and not of evil, to give you a future and a hope.' (Jeremiah 29:11).**

Greatness, many a times is attained through adversities. The Bible recalls that Jesus endured suffering because of the glory ahead. That is why you must 'see' the greatness - your preferred future – to be sufficiently motivated to 'die' for it.

'Jesus said, most assuredly, I say to you, unless a grain of wheat falls into the ground and dies, it

remains alone; but if it dies, it produces much grain.'

I John 12:24

Described in the Bible as a 'Treasure', greatness is within you. It is important to remember that we are human beings with frailties. 2 Corinthians 4:7 tells us: ***'But we have this treasure in earthen vessels that the excellence of power may be of God not of us'***

While hard work, diligence, focus are important requirements for attaining greatness, yet, God wants us to depend on Him for help, *not our human ability. . .* ***'that the excellence of power may be of God not of us.'*** God never likes to share His glory with anyone! What is this treasure? It is the *life* of Christ in us but hidden in our fallen human nature. How does this treasure get uncovered? Because it is hidden in an earthen vessel, it gets uncovered as the vessel is broken! The breaking process is described in verses 10, 11 as participation in the death and resurrection of our Lord Jesus. As we humbly submit to the death of Christ, allowing God to break our earthiness (clay pot) through suffering, adversities, and trials, we are able to manifest the life of Jesus, exuding His sweet aroma! Paul describes these sufferings as 'affliction, 'perplexity, and persecution and being struck down.' This death reveals the hidden treasure in us which is the life of Christ. Paul describes it this way:

'We are hard-pressed on every side, yet not crushed; we are perplexed, but not in despair; persecuted, but not forsaken; struck down, but not destroyed— always carrying about in the body the dying of the Lord Jesus, that the life of Jesus also may be manifested in our body. For we who live are always delivered to death for Jesus' sake, that the life of Jesus also may be manifested in our mortal flesh. So then death is working in us, but life in you.'

2 Corinthians 4:8-12

The more you see that treasure in you, the more Christ's brilliance shines forth in you. And in the midst of your earthiness, God gets the glory as you yourself are transformed from glory to glory!

Chapter Seven

My Encouragement to You

'But as many as received Him, to them He gave the right to <u>become</u> children of God, to those who believe in His name'

John 1:12 (NKJV)

You have read this book thus far because there's a hunger in you, a desire for more. Congratulations! Your desire shall be met as the Lord lives. But, on the other hand, you are overwhelmed or perhaps, you feel guilty by your inadequacies and failures. You placed yourself beside "the woman of substance" portrayed in this book and you did not measure up. Let me remind you, God is not looking for perfect people, rather, He is looking for willing people.

Are you willing to make the effort required to change so you can become a fulfilled woman? Are you so willing you are even prepared to forego some things in replacement of the REAL THING? If your answers to these questions are 'yes', you are on the right path. Go for it girl! Besides all the help and resources around you, you have a divine Helper who can never fail nor disappoint you!

Let me encourage you further. Do you realize that Jesus, as Man experienced all our travails. Like us, He was tempted at every point; '*seeing then that we have a High Priest who has passed through the heavens, Jesus the Son of God. . .*'

Hebrews 4:14

Again, like us He learned to obey:

'**though He was a Son, yet He learned obedience by the things which He suffered.**'

Hebrews 5:8

Jesus also made some choices intentionally because He constantly focused on His purpose and was being guided by His purpose. '**Now my soul is troubled, and what shall I say? 'Father, save Me from this hour'? But for this purpose I came to this hour. Father, glorify Your name.'** (John 12:27-28)

The same path He threaded, we also must thread. Because He did not fail, our success is guaranteed, if we follow after Him.

So, you can be great! You can live a purposeful, happy life. Perhaps there are bad habits you have been trying so hard to get rid of, habits such as feelings of bad temperament, bitterness, distrust, anger, jealousy, self-sabotaging utterances, and the like. Do not condemn yourself for being earthen. Don't try to "cast out" your 'earthiness' either. Just realize that you have Christ "The Treasure" in you. Remember you are earthen and will always be! But, as you keep your focus on Jesus, you will be transformed into His image.

Lastly, it is stated in the Bible that,

'But as many as received Him, to them He gave the right to become children of God, to those who believe in His name'

John 1:12

Isn't it liberating to know we are called 'to become' not 'being' children of God. There is hope for you as there is for me. Even, if up until now, you have failed in your attempts to live a worthy life, you can start again, knowing that you *become* your best, one day at a time...

Reflection Time
with
Women of Substance

Chapter Eight

Reflection Time with Women of Substance

Q: **How do women within your sphere of influence come across to you? (Please define your sphere of influence - professional, artisans, University lecturers, church or diverse? If diverse, please give a brief description of their composition).**

A: My sphere of influence right now is the church. However, on account of the need to be able to function in an aggressively non-Christian environment, at times, I use the professional angle by way of introduction. I am a Geologist by Training. Lectured and then ran a Geological Consultancy for a total of 19 years before God called me into full time ministry in 1994. So occasionally, I go by the professional appellation to gain access to some spheres.

Women in my sphere of influence relate with me in a variety of ways. Some as a mother, who is over them, and from whom they receive mentoring, while others see me as a senior who is blazing a trail ahead of them. To the glory of God, the Missionary assignment God gave to me through the Church, had never been given to a woman before in The Redeemed Christian Church of God. I was called into full time ministry in 1994 and appointed as a Regional Controller.

This involves crossing borders with the gospel of the kingdom, planting churches and raising ministers to run same. There is yet another group of women I am sorry to say, who do not really like me. I want to believe it might be a combination of envy, and a spirit of competition. However, I am always mindful that God is the One who has defined our destinies. In order to fulfill it, God determines when and where you are needed.

Also, within my sphere of influence, the women I also invariably relate with are ministry heads. That is, female General Overseers. On account of the magnitude of mandate reposed on me by virtue of my assignment, there is a greater level of acceptance and ability to relate with these female Church Leaders.

Q: **What is your perspective of a WOMAN OF SUBSTANCE? Who is she? Who can she become?**

A: She is someone who has made Jesus her anchor. You really cannot achieve much of a lasting nature, without a personal relationship, and constant, consistent and intimate relationship with Jesus. A woman of substance must of necessity live by integrity. She must be able to hold her head high. Otherwise she may be misunderstood to have reached where she is at by favoritism, rather than by merit and the favor of God. She must be competent in her profession or calling whatever it may be.

A woman of substance must be very sensitive spiritually. Usually she will be a threat to some others including men. My experience shows that people would also want to trip her up, just to prove that she is not all she claims to be. So sensitivity of spirit is necessary in order to avoid pit falls and traps. As God is helping her, this woman must remain humble. She, woman must see God as her Source of all things. She must not make the quest for money her number one priority. This implies that she must obey all the principles of God with respect to tithing, giving, and be ready to sow sacrificially. She may at first appear foolish to those watching. However, she is sowing into her future. As the harvest begins to come and the substance begins to manifest in every sense, nobody will be able to say they made Abraham rich!!!! She will have God and God alone to thank for the glory that now shows over her life.

A woman of substance lives by excellence. By the way she carries herself; you will find that without any advertisement, her life makes a statement. In her dressing, her manner of speaking, her spiritual life, especially what you perceive of her in public etc. you can tell that you are not dealing with a mere woman so to speak.

Q. **As a senior, mentoring younger generations of women, what is your counsel and advice to such groups growing up to become women of substance?**

A. **My counsel to the younger woman coming up are these:**

- Wait your turn. Do not push, manipulate or lobby for anything. At the appointed time God will lift you up.

- Take the time before your manifestation, to learn as much as you can form those ahead of you. Learn from their strengths and their weaknesses.

- Do not play the comparison game. The plan of God for each life is different. Apostle Paul has counseled that they comparing themselves with themselves, measuring themselves against themselves are not wise.

- Be someone who is teachable. Be open to correction. You do not know it all. You are not perfect. You can also not be the only one right all the time.

- Be a giver. Practice giving as a way of life and honor those above you. Submit to them, help them succeed. Then God will raise up helpers for you too who will help you succeed as well.

I have found that if you refuse to go anywhere empty handed including church, God will always put in your hands that which you can give. The Woman of Substance also has to maintain and sustain that position. By the time you reach a top or senior position, do not stop doing the things that God used to get you where you are.

Q: Any other comments.

A: Continue to grow in your relationship with God. Do not become obnoxious as some women tend to do once they become seemingly powerful. Never lower the honor and esteem you give to your husband. You are a complement to and not competition for him. You have no point to prove. Also do not neglect your children and their needs just because you are now well known. God will ask of them from you.

Pastor Margaret Oluwatosin Macauley is the Regional Coordinator, North Central Africa Region, with Headquarters in Addis Ababa, Ethiopia. The Region comprises the following countries:

Ethiopia, Republic of South Sudan, (Khartoum), Republic of Sudan (Juba), Republic of Djibouti, and Eritrea. I am a Missionary with the Redeemed Christian Church of God and also the first woman missionary to be sent out by the church. Other women on the field are working alongside their husbands.

Q: How do women within your sphere of influence come across to you? (Please define your sphere of influence - professional, artisans, University lecturers, church or diverse? If diverse, please give a brief description of their composition).

A: The women involved in my sphere of influence have varied over the years. The variation has been largely based on what phase of life I have been in. In my early years, the women of influence have included my mother, grandmothers and aunts, who were all women of great faith in God. The phase where I was in Medical school and Residency training provided me with women who were in private practice or teaching Faculty. In more recent years, as a Pastor assisting my husband in ministry, the women in my sphere of influence have mostly included women in similar positions as me. Such women of influence have portrayed themselves as Christian women of honorable character and with great knowledge of the Bible. They are women of resolute faith, confidence and humility.

Q: What is your perspective of a **WOMAN OF SUBSTANCE?** Who is she? Who can she become?

91

A woman of substance is a Christian woman of great worth, character, and wisdom. The qualities of such a woman include: patience, honesty, integrity, peacefulness and love, to name a few. She is a humble woman, who knows her limitations and weaknesses and is able to learn from them by playing up her strengths. There is a sense of quiet confidence and strength about her.

A woman of substance is knowledgeable about many things, both secular and biblical. She keeps herself aware of the current events happening around her (neighborhood, city, country, and worldwide etc.) and she endeavors to support where it is needed and she is able.

She may have endured some trials or hardships during the course of her life but she has been able to overcome and rise above them, which in the long run has strengthened and matured her. Such a woman probably has a hobby or outside interests, and her happiness and significance is not tied to her job or her husband.

Despite having a somewhat independent spirit, a woman of substance values her family and everything that is involved in this sacred unit. She values the relationship with her husband and her children, and will do anything possible to keep it together.

Most importantly, a woman of substance is steadfast in her faith to God. Her life is not shallow and not solely dependent on the 'here and now', knowing that many of the cares of this world will soon fade away and be replaced by an eternal glory. She is keenly aware that her tomorrow will be alright. For such a woman of substance, the potential to advance is great. There are no limitations as to where she can go or who she could become.

Pastor Manita Fadele: A pastor, pastor's wife and Medical Practitioner.

Q: How do women within your sphere of influence come across to you? (Please define your sphere of influence - professional, artisans, University lecturers, church or diverse? If diverse, please give a brief description of their composition).

A: Sphere of Influence: Basically, they are women in the church or in church-related activities. They are of varied race, profession and economic status. But, as a pastor and pastor's wife, I relate with a lot of women who like me are either pastors or pastors' wives.

Q: What is your perspective of a **WOMAN OF SUBSTANCE?** Who is she? Who can she become?

A: A woman of substance is described in Proverbs 31. She knows how to take care of her family, no matter what the circumstance is, she is willing to do whatever it takes to see their needs met. Working and raising a family is not an issue, she can balance both. A woman of substance is a woman of power, a woman of positive influence and a woman of meaning. To be branded a woman of substance is one of the greatest compliments one can give a woman that wants to be an 'influential' female.

Q: As a senior, mentoring younger generations of women, what is your counsel and advice to such groups on growing up to become women of substance?

A: Know your purpose!

Pastor Sheila Bowling - Pastor - Eagle Rock Church, Founder of Gritty Women of God and also founder of Kingdom Kids (preschool/daycare) and Eagle Preparatory School (Kindergarten – 12th grade)

People of my scope of influence can reach me without any problem; I'm open to people of all ages, color and race. As a pastor you influence a lot of professionals, all kinds of people. A woman of substance in my own definition is a woman who has surrendered to the Lord, born again genuinely and serving Him. A woman of substance is a submissive person first to God and to her own husband. She can be anything that God created her to be (in the RCCG) you can become a Pastor, parish, area, zonal, provincial, special assistant, God has blessed us richly, the sky is not even her limit as they say .My advice is that we serve The Lord acceptably don't lack behind in anything you do, commitment is the key, be committed to whatever you are doing secularly or spiritually. And bear in mind that there is a reward for you, from The Lord.

Pastor Margaret Adeyokunnu: A Pastor, Pastor's wife Member of RCCG Church Family, North America.

```
`````````````````````````````````````````````````````````````````
```

*Q:* How do women within your sphere of influence come across to you? (Please define your sphere of influence - professional, artisans, University lecturers, church or diverse? If diverse, please give a brief description of their composition).
```

A: My sphere of influence is diverse: I interact with women from various backgrounds. Some of them are very lettered, having acquired a minimum of first degree, university education. Some have only school certificate level of education and some are illiterates. There are also in my sphere of influence those who are professionals and university lecturers, public service officers, caterers, fashion designers, shop attendants, semi-illiterate farmers, full time home makers, single mothers and those in pastoral works with their husbands. I think it would be more appropriate to say that my interaction with women cut across a wide spectrum of society, transcending educational, geographic, linguistic, religio-socio-economic backgrounds.

As varied as the shapes, sizes and backgrounds of these women are, there are common threads that run through them all. I would classify them using the Bell curve model. A relatively small number, who are consciously aware of:

- Who they are as women,
- Their spiritually endowed role in the grand scheme of things, in other words, of their higher role in creation.

At the other end of the spectrum is another small number, who are only aware of their material existence. The majority falls in the middle – those who are struggling to understand the purpose of their existence and their role in creation.

Q: What is your perspective of a WOMAN OF SUBSTANCE? Who is she? Who can she become?

A: It is quite a challenge to give written expression to this concept. When I was much younger I would not have hesitated to put pen to paper and write volumes about the so-called woman of substance. Today, I'm more circumspect and reticent. It is hard for me to think about a woman without substance for that would run counter to creation. It is utterly inconceivable that there can be anything created or to be created without substance. The creator can attest to this. I do not think that the creator will consider his/her creation as being without substance.

I recall the story I read about a Sudanese girl, whose name I do not recall. By some fortuitous turn of events, she left the poverty and squalor of her homeland and became a successful model in the United States. The image of the turmoil and suffering back home was well etched in her memory. Intending to alleviate her mother's pain and suffering, she brought her some money. Her mother rejected the money because in her consciousness it was made from shameful means. In her paradigm, her daughter had lost 'substance'. The daughter's chagrin was deep and palpable.

Would the daughter conclude that her mother has 'substance' and she does not?

Conversely, there is the story of Oluchi, the Nigerian girl, who won the first MNET face of Africa and became a world renowned model. Like her Sudanese counterpart, she brought money home and raised her parents from poverty and squalor. What were the thoughts of her parents before and after their daughter attained stardom? It is the general practice in Nigeria that the pride of place is accorded the male not the female child. So, if we assume that Oluchi's parents did not think a daughter had 'substance', is there likelihood that those views would be substantially modified if not altogether changed after she gained stardom?

A comparison of the reactions of both parents would reveal the differences in their levels of consciousness, which is a manifestation of the thoughts held and choices made in life.

The foregoing examples serve to illustrate the point that the word substance loses its substance when it comes face to face with the substance of existence.

Q: As a senior, mentoring younger generations of women, what is your counsel and advice to such groups on growing up to become women of substance?

Q. Believe in yourself. You are a unique individual. There is not a second person like you in the universe. Find out what you can contribute to make humanity better. If you were to experience transition today, what would people say you contributed to make their lives better? There is something, which you and only you can birth on this plane. Others can give you good counsel but the ultimate decision to use it and take responsibility for the outcome lies with you.

There is no reinventing the wheel. People have travelled this route before you and others will come after you. Learn from the experiences of others but personalize it by adding your unique flavor. One is never too old to learn. The mind that keeps seeking and learning never grows old. Learn to discern form from substance.

Any other comments?

What makes one a woman? Is it the fact of being a female? We must know some females, who do not share any of the accepted female roles just like we know some men, who are more effeminate than the female. This situation is more glaring in a single sex relationship where one partner clearly exhibits roles usually assigned to his/her heterosexual counterparts. Is being born the female of the Homo Sapiens a *fait accompli*, a sealed box?

When does a woman become a mother – the day she gives birth to her baby? Can a woman, who cannot bear a child be a mother? As humans, we are limited in our scope of understanding. But if we care to observe Nature, we will broaden our span of vision and understanding. I'll like to share a story that happened in our household in 1982. We had a dog and several cats. One of the cats had a litter but died shortly after. We were all concerned about how to keep the kittens alive. We bought baby milk and feeding bottles with teats. Unfortunately, the teats were too large for the kittens. Our concern turned into worry. The next thing I knew was that our dog, Brownie, not a bitch, had developed teats and kittens were suckling him. Brownie took care of the kittens as their mother would have done.

Growing up, we learnt that cats would not eat from the same plate as dogs so we served their meals in separate plates. We discovered to our amazement that the kittens that Brownie nursed preferred to start eating from his plate and he would stay aside for them to finish before helping himself to his meal.

Once upon a time in my life I would have been content to just label the experience as a miracle and give it no further thought. Knowing that what we term miracle is the manifestation of a higher law in our material realm, I pondered long and deep for a possible understanding of why a dog would develop teats to nurse kittens. Unexpectedly one day, I had the intuitive flash that Nature was cooperating with our intention to support and sustain life and the dog evolved to meet the challenge of the moment. I came to the conclusion that Nature does not create the rigid boundaries, which we mortals erect. Nature will allow the evolution of man or woman in accordance with the exigencies of the moment, which we have to deal with for our survival and spiritual evolution.

The biological fact of being born a woman is a potential capable of evolving into myriads of possibilities in accordance with the functions and roles she is called upon to perform in life. She can limit the possibilities based on the thoughts and choices she makes and ultimately her level of consciousness. As her consciousness expands and she becomes more aware of herself and the role of the female in Creation, and makes a conscious choice to cooperate with Nature in that role, Nature will empower her to make manifest her endowment as a woman to help humanity to grow. This is evolution for her and humanity. Individually and collectively, humanity's strive for growth is in an upward spiral. This growth is more spiritual than physical. Since 'no one throws pearls at swine' Nature will only ennoble and empower the evolved woman to carry out this noble role for and on behalf of the Universe. No limitation can therefore be placed on such a woman. She can become anything and everything she wills to become.

Oladunni Olasehan is a multi-skilled, multi-talented and multi-tasking individual, who believes that one is not too old to learn and like a child, she's excited to discover each day a new petal that opens up to her in her quest for self-discovery and self-realization. A retired banker with approximately 26 years of experience; human resources specialist, Oladunni is also a student of philosophy and metaphysics, speaks and writes English and French, edits books, magazines and journals and video recordings. She is a Fashion designer and the Distinguished Toastmasters Award holder - the highest award bestowed by Toastmasters International.

Q: How do women within your sphere of influence come across to you? (Please define your sphere of influence - professional, artisans, University lecturers, church or diverse? If diverse, please give a brief description of their composition).

A: My interaction with women varies, as a pastors wife my sphere of influence include women in my church and in my community. I spend most of my time encouraging, mentoring, and praying for the women in my inner circle, within my congregation, and around the world. I find this aspect of my pastoral work very rewarding.

Q: What is your perspective of a WOMAN OF SUBSTANCE? Who is she? Who can she become?

Q: A woman of substance is God's leading lady, she knows who and whose she is. She is confident in herself, and knows her purpose. As a woman of substance, she is determined to fulfill her destiny and walk in greatness.

Q: **As a senior, mentoring younger generations of women, what is your counsel and advice to such groups on growing up to become women of substance?**

Q: Learn from other women of substance.

Any other comments?

Since God is a God of purpose and He is the one that created man and woman in His image. God has purpose for a man, also does for a woman. A woman's purpose can be defined by WHO she is Christ Jesus however, their purpose can be found as a mother, a sister, a counselor, a preacher, a leader, and a role model to people around her.

Pastor (Mrs.) Modupe Sanusi, Co-Pastor at RCCG Restoration Chapel, Houston, TX; and the author of 'Marriage Rx: 10 Prescription for a Happy Marriage.'

Comments by a few men...

Q: How do women within your sphere of influence come across to you? (Please define your sphere of influence - professional, artisans, University lecturers, church or diverse?. If diverse, please give a brief description of their composition).

Q • I'm a Pastor and a Business man, so I interact with a varied spectra of women both in the Church and business world.

• As a pastor, I work with female ministers, ministry leaders and members of the congregation. In terms of women of substance, I can say that these women come across to me as women who are capable, competent, energized, driven, spirit-filled, intelligent, motivated, dedicated, compassionate, supportive of the ministry and women who can pretty much tackle as much a challenge (if not more) as any of my male ministers, ministry leaders or members of the congregation.

• I also work with women as a business man and find most of the qualities already mentioned above to be true in that regard also.

Q: What is your perspective of a WOMAN OF SUBSTANCE? Who is she? Who can she become?

Q • A Woman of Substance is a woman who is visionary, focused, professional, and deeply spiritual (i.e. connected to God through Christ). She is a woman who is gifted, hardworking, creative and compassionate, she is a person who is strong and yet exudes a heart of care and compassion. She must be sensitive, eager to serve others, respectful of others and mostly her husband (if married). Must be able to run her own home and uphold family values, She is able to hold up under adversity and is an encourager.

• A Woman of Substance can become whatever her heart sets out to become with God being the central focus of her life!

• As a senior, mentoring the younger generation, what is your counsel and advise to such group growing up to become a WOMAN OF SUBSTANCE?

Q: **My advice to the younger generation of women who desire to become Women of Substance is as follows:**

Q • Get connected with God – He is the one that can help to draw out the substance that He has deposited in you

• Separate yourself from any suggestion that women are incapable of achieving much in life

• Surround yourself with fellow women and men who encourage you to become the woman of substance that God has called you to be

- Study the lives of older women of substance and peers whom you admire and emulate key aspects of their lifestyle
- Develop the core of your person, by discovering you strengths, gifts and qualities that can make you to become a Woman of Substance and work on them.
- Start from where you are; be faithful even in little things
- Trust God to make you into what he has ordained for you to be.

Any other comments?

I'm glad that you have embarked on writing a book of this nature; I believe it will be an encouragement to many women everywhere!

Pastor Ghandi Olaoye, Senior Pastor RCCG, Jesus House, DC.

Q. **How do women within your sphere of influence come across to you? (Please define your sphere of influence - professional, artisans, University lecturers, church or diverse? If diverse, please give a brief description of their composition).**

A. I meet with many women in my sphere of influence being a Parish Pastor. Most of these women have something in common which is caring and worrying about their families. A lot of them however, in doing this, tend to be focused on improving their economic situations.

Q: **What is your perspective of a WOMAN OF SUBSTANCE? Who is she? Who can she become?**

A: Being a woman of substance means being influential, having something to give rather than looking to take. It means always being ready to improve on what is so as to realize what can be rather than maintaining the status quo. I strongly believe every woman should look inwards and aspire to be the best they can be and refuse to be limited. They should know they have as much room to grow as their male counterparts.

**Pastor Tola Odutola, Senior Pastor RCCG,
Jesus House Baltimore, MD.**

I am a military man by profession and by and large, this restricts my interaction with people. Generally, my interaction within and outside the military is diverse and it is basically determined by a number of issues that define my personality and beliefs. Some of the issues are faith based, sincerity, openness, mannerism amongst others but certainly does not include status, tribal, class or religious sentiments.

A Woman of Substance is that woman that epitomizes all or most of the virtues listed in Proverbs 31:10-27. Additionally, she is respectful, ever willing to forgive as well as amenable to training and correction etc.

She can aspire and attain to any position in accordance with God's calling upon her life. She should be a living good example to other women, ladies or co-workers irrespective of gender and these group of people should be able to look up to her for mentoring.

A Woman of Substance should keep her light shining constantly, radiating the beauty of Christ, guiding others with love, evangelizing those she comes across through her way of life as was testified of Ruth in Ruth 3:11 as well as guiding those coming after her to attain their full God-given potentials.

Colonel Kunle Adesope,
Defense Attaché, Nigerian Embassy Cairo, Egypt.

Closing Remarks

If this book has blessed you in any way, particularly, if while reading the book you said in your heart, 'I want to know you Lord' or 'I want you in my life' or 'I want to become a woman of substance' , please say this simple prayer;

'Heavenly Father, I thank you. I really don't know you but I want to know you better. Please reveal Jesus to me personally. I invite you into my heart, come and reign in my life. Be my Lord and Savior, forgive all my sins and lead me to the path of greatness which you have ordained for me. I thank you for answering my prayers. I pray in Jesus name. Amen.'

If you truly prayed this prayer from your heart, you can contact the author at wos.book@gmail.com or visit our website at www.gloryandvirtuemin.org

Remain blessed.

About the Author

Pastor (Mrs.) Bimpe Ishola, is a skillful teacher, trainer, life-coach, and mentor with a God-endowed gift of prayer. She is a practical speaker who draws from her life experiences and training. As a mother and wife, she also has a growing desire to promote healthy family relationships by raising prayerful strong women of virtue, grace and substance. She has been a guest speaker at many Women Conferences in Nigeria, United States of America and Canada.

Pastor Bimpe's passion for teaching the word of God is expressed in her ministry - LEADERSHIP TRAINING & DEVELOPMENT. She has over 25 year experience as a teacher and trainer in secular and biblical knowledge. She has A Bachelor's Degree in Education, Master's Degree in

Industrial/Organizational Psychology and Dip. Theology. Pastor Bimpe is the Founder/Chief Servant Officer of Glory & Virtue Ministries, a ministry she founded in 2005 with a mission to disciple believers to be the best they can be for God. Also founded by her is the WOMEN OF SUBSTANCE INTERNATIONAL – an organization that challenges women and encourages the development of their potentials. As an administrator, Pastor Bimpe is currently the Registrar of Redeemer's Leadership Institute, an institute with a mandate to develop quality leadership and accountability.

Currently, Pastor Bimpe assists her husband in building God's kingdom at RCCG Triumphant Chapel Columbus Ohio while also pastoring RCCG Winners' Assembly, Delaware, Ohio. She resides in Columbus Ohio with her family.

In August 2003, a journalist with a local Christian Magazine interviewed Pastor Bimpe Ishola after the historic event of February when she organized a women rally to take over Ikorodu town for Christ. Below are the excerpts of the interview:

A WOMAN OF EXCELLENCE

'She hails from Oyo State, one out of nine children. She was born into the Christian family of Mr. and Mrs. Emmanuel Aderohunmu Adesokan. She has 5 sisters and 3 brothers, among them are a set of twins. She completed both her primary and secondary education in Oyo State. She completed her A-levels and then went on to university where she graduated in 1981. She left her state of origin to Enugu for N.Y.S.C. She worked briefly as a Teacher/Counselor with the Federal Civil Service. She went back to the University to study Industrial/Organizational Psychology. On completion of her studies, she joined Afribank Plc., in 1984.

Four months before now, Asst. Pastor (Mrs.) Bimpe Ishola was the Branch Manager of Afribank Plc., Ikorodu Branch, and also the first female Area Pastor of the Redeemed Christian Church of God (RCCG), Lagos Province 2, Acme Rd., Ikeja.

She became born again at the Scripture Pasture Christian Center (SPCC) in 1986. Her hunger to be fed with the word of God grew and her new experience led her to RCCG, Ebutte-Metta. She became a member in 1987. In 1990, she joined the model parish at Ladipo Oluwole, from there to Acme family and later to Overcomers' Parish, Ikorodu in 1995. She was the pioneer Parish Pastor of New Wine Parish, Ikorodu in 1998.Precisely three years later, she became the Area Pastor of Area 38, New Wine Parish having become the Area Headquarters on September 1 2002. What were her challenges as the first female Area Pastor in the Province?

According to her, 'Being the first female Area Pastor in the Province, all eyes are on you. For me to be chosen as an Area Pastor means they have confidence in me to perform, therefore I will try my best by the grace of God not to disappoint the people and most importantly, the Almighty God.' Her challenges include coordinating the Area which consists of different parishes and to improve on the set standard. Her relationship with the parish pastors under her was cordial. The pastors were understanding and cooperative and she also shared her burdens with some of her ministers.

Under her, Area 38 started with four parishes, viz:- Power Assembly, New Wine Parish, Resurrection Center and Latter House, but has now increased to seven with the Jubilee

Parish , King of Glory and the Kings of Pavilion; plus two mission fields: Agufoye and Olodo mission fields. Indeed Area 38 is a model Area.

Asst. Pastor (Mrs.) Bimpe Ishola was able to combine her ministerial and secular job together by the special grace of God and the support of her loving and understanding husband, who is her confidant and her counselor. According to her, the peaceful atmosphere in her home front and the ability to understand and manage people very well also contributed to the success.

Her role model and mentor is first and foremost, the Almighty God, followed by our Mother-in-Israel, Pastor (Mrs.) Foluke Adeboye. Other role models are Pastor (Mrs.) Yemisi Adeloye and a woman in her former place of work who is upright and diligent. Her advice and word of encouragement to the women folk is that we should not see our sex as a limitation to what we aspire to do. Being the weaker sex is not an excuse to be lazy, because the reasons why we are excused will be used against us in the time of advancement. We should be focused. The feminine gender should harness our God-given potential. Lastly, we should be committed in the place of prayer.

A/P (Mrs.) Bimpe Ishola is a woman of integrity who does not compromise her faith, diligence and honesty. She is indeed very humble and realizes the fact that the way to the top is really the way of humility.'

Bimbola Kelani
Trumpet of Jubilee Magazine, August 2003

Notes